O9-ABH-691

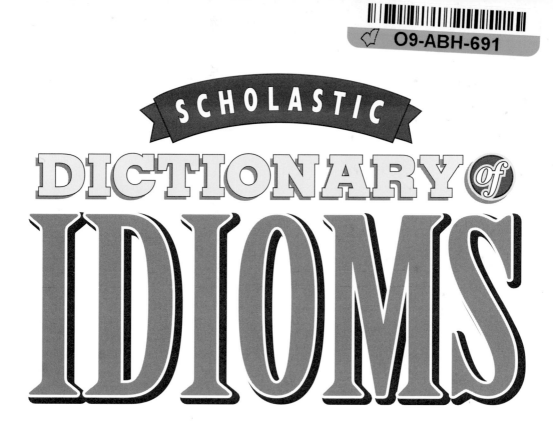

SCHOLASTIC

DICTIONARY of

IDIOMS

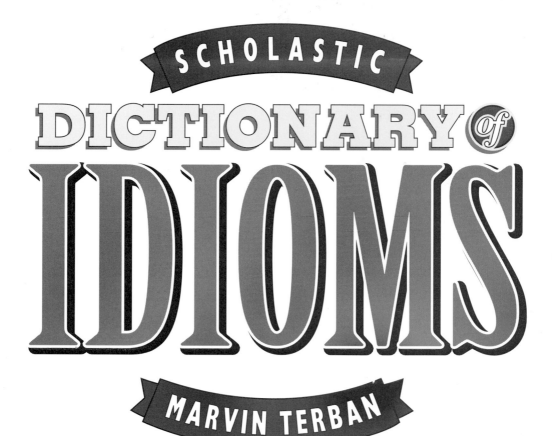

SCHOLASTIC
DICTIONARY of IDIOMS

MARVIN TERBAN

SCHOLASTIC
REFERENCE

New York Toronto London Auckland Sydney

Design:	Karen Hudson
Illustration:	John Devore
Production:	Kevin Callahan

No part of this publication may be reproduced in whole or in part, or stored in a retrieval system, or transmitted in any form or by any means, electronic, mechanical, photocopying, recording or otherwise, without written permission of the publisher. For information regarding permission, write to Scholastic Inc., 555 Broadway, New York, New York 10012.

ISBN 0-590-27552-6

Copyright © 1996 by Scholastic Inc.
All rights reserved. Published by Scholastic Inc.

12 11 10 9 8 7 6 5 4   12   7 8 9/9 0 1/0

Printed in the U.S.A.   09

INTRODUCTION

What are idioms?

Idioms appear in every language, and English has thousands of them. They are often confusing because the meaning of the whole group of words taken together has little, often nothing, to do with the meanings of the words taken one by one.

For instance, to "let the cat out of the bag" means to reveal a secret. Today the phrase has nothing to do with a cat or a bag, but hundreds of years ago, it actually did.

In order to understand a language, you must know what the idioms in that language mean. If you try to figure out the meaning of an idiom literally, word by word, you will get befuddled. You have to know its "hidden" meaning.

⇨

Where did all these idioms come from?

Idioms come from all different sources, from the Bible to horse racing, from ancient fables to modern slang. Sometimes famous authors and storytellers such as Homer, Aesop, Geoffrey Chaucer, or William Shakespeare made them up to add spark to their writings. The authors were popular, so the expressions they created became popular. Often, however, we don't know the name of the first author or speaker who used a particular expression.

Some idioms came from Native-American customs ("bury the hatchet") and others from African-American speech ("chill out"). Some became popular because they rhyme ("snug as a bug in a rug") or have alliteration ("spick and span").

Some idioms originated as colloquialisms (informal speech) or slang (casual, playful, non-standard language). Some were well-known proverbs and adages (short sayings that express practical, basic truths). Some popular idioms began as folksy sayings used in particular regions of the country and spoken in local dialects. Many came from other countries, although most of the idioms in this book are Americanisms. Some idioms go back in time to the ancient Greeks and Romans, thousands of years ago. Others are more recent.

Word experts who study origins of idiomatic expressions don't always agree on exactly where each one came from. In this book, I've included the most accepted explanations.

What is a cliché?

If an expression becomes overused, we call it a cliché, and many of the sayings in this book are clichés. Once these expressions were fresh and original, but today they are stale and trite. You should try to avoid using clichés in your own writing (unless you can put an imaginative new twist on them), but you will hear and read clichés all the time.

What's in this book?

This book will explain the meanings and origins behind more than 600 idioms that you might hear or read in English every day. Our panel of teachers helped me choose the most commonly confusing idioms.

English is a beautiful and rich language, but its many idioms are often tough nuts to crack. This Dictionary of Idioms should help make understanding these sayings as easy as pie.

Marvin Terban

The following educators carefully reviewed the master list of idioms and gave invaluable suggestions regarding the content of this book:

Joni Chadkin
Bilingual Elementary School Teacher
Los Angeles, California

Kimberly Colen
Children's Book Author
Dallas, Texas

Raul Hernandez
Cecilia Walker
English as a Second Language Teachers
Key West, Florida

Bobbie and David Hobson
Fifth Grade Teachers
Boise, Idaho

Marianne Pei
Elementary/Middle School Librarian
New York, New York

Burrell Ross
High School Principal (retired)
Los Lunas, New Mexico

Becky Shepard
Reading Specialist
Burlington, Massachusetts

Grateful acknowledgement is made to Barbara Kipfer, Ph. D., for bringing her lexicographical expertise to the *Scholastic Dictionary of Idioms*.

For my wife, Karen

Idiomatically and alphabetically, she is the Apple of my eye,
Bright eyed and bushy tailed, Cool as a cucumber,
Down to earth, an Eager beaver, and Full of beans.
She has a Green thumb, a Heart of gold, and she's always
In the pink. She's a Jack of all trades,
Keeps a stiff upper lip, always Lends an ear and
Minds her p's and q's. She's Nothing to sneeze at,
On the ball, the Power behind the throne, and
Quick on the uptake. She Runs rings around others,
is a Sight for sore eyes, and always Tickles my funny bone.
She's Up to date, Very va-va-voom, Worth her salt,
extraordinarily Young at heart and Zingy.

HOW TO USE THIS DICTIONARY

This dictionary is organized from A to Z. If you are looking for the meaning or origin of an idiom, you can begin by looking under the first letter of the first word of that idiom. For example, the idiom "throw a monkey wrench into the works" can be found under the letter T.

But what if you know only one or two words of an idiom? You're in luck! At the back of this book, all the idioms are indexed both alphabetically and also by key words. In the Key Word Index, "Throw a monkey wrench into the works" also can be found under "throw" or "monkey" or "wrench" or "works."

Many idioms are similar in meaning. Sometimes, an idiom is included in the entry for another, similar idiom. When you look it up, it will say, "*See*—" and show another idiom to turn to. There is no separate entry for this idiom, but reading about the other, similar idiom can guide you.

Whether you've been speaking English all your life or are just learning, this book can help you read and speak with new understanding and a lot more fun!

Ace up Your Sleeve

"I don't know how Henry is going to get his mom to buy him a bike, but I'm sure he has an ace up his sleeve."

Meaning: a surprise or secret advantage, especially something tricky that is kept hidden until needed

Origin: Back in the 1500s most people didn't have pockets in their clothes, so they kept things in their sleeves. Later on, magicians hid objects, even small live animals, up their sleeves and then pulled them out unexpectedly to surprise their audiences. In the 1800s dishonest card players secretly slipped a winning card, often an ace, up their sleeves and pulled it out when nobody was looking to win the game.

Achilles' Heel

I'm an A student in math and science, but English is my Achilles' heel.

Meaning: the one weakness, fault, flaw, or vulnerable spot in one's otherwise strong character

Origin: In the *Iliad,* the famous story about the Trojan War by the Greek poet Homer, Achilles was a great hero and warrior. However, he had one weak spot, the heel of one foot. When he was a baby, his mother wanted to be certain that her son could never be harmed, so she dipped little Achilles upside-down in the magical River Styx. Wherever the water touched his body, he became invulnerable. But since she was holding him by his heel, that part of him never got wet. Years later Achilles was killed in the Trojan War by an enemy who shot a poisoned arrow into his heel.

Add Fuel to the Fire

"I was already angry with you, and when you forgot to pick me up, that really added fuel to the fire."

Meaning: to make a bad situation worse; to do or say something that causes more trouble, makes someone angrier

Origin: Thousands of years ago the famous Roman historian Livy used this expression. If you pour water on a fire, it goes out. But if you put fuel (like coal or wood) on a fire, you make it burn hotter and brighter. If "fire" represents any kind of trouble, then anything you do to make that trouble worse is "fuel." A similar expression is "fan the flames."

Air Your Dirty Laundry in Public

> My upstairs neighbors fight a lot and air their dirty laundry in public.

Meaning: to talk about your private disagreements or embarrassing matters in public, usually while quarreling

Origin: Picture this: Instead of hanging your freshly washed laundry on a clothesline, you hang your dirty clothes out there in the air for all the world to see. Wouldn't that be embarrassing? Imagine that your "dirty laundry" represents secret personal matters and that "to air" them means to discuss them out loud for anyone to hear. Some people use "air your dirty linen in public."

Albatross around Your Neck

"Everywhere I go, my mother makes me take my little bratty sister. She's an albatross around my neck."

Meaning: a very difficult burden that you can't get rid of or a reminder of something you did that was wrong

Origin: In 1798 the English poet Samuel Taylor Coleridge wrote his most famous poem, "The Rime of the Ancient Mariner." In the poem a young sailor shoots a large seabird called an albatross. In those days that was considered very unlucky. Sure enough, a lot of bad things happen to the ship, and the crew blames the young sailor. They hang the dead bird around his neck.

All Ears

"You said you had something important to tell me. I'm all ears!"

Meaning: eager to listen; sharply attentive; curious

Origin: The ear is the organ by which a person hears. So, if we figuratively say that you're "all ears," it means that at that moment you're keenly listening to whatever is being said. It's as if no other part of your body mattered except your ears. This idiom is about three centuries old.

All Thumbs

"Marco can't build the model of the atom for the science project. He's all thumbs."

Meaning: awkward and clumsy, especially with the hands

Origin: Human beings and apes have thumbs; most other animals don't. A thumb helps the other fingers pick things up, turn dials, and do other fine motor tasks. But what if all your fingers were thumbs? You'd have a hard time picking up small objects, keyboarding a computer, doing art projects, and so on. That's why this expression means clumsy at doing physical tasks with your hands.

Ants in Your Pants

"You never sit still. You must have ants in your pants."

Meaning: extreme restlessness; overactivity

Origin: We can easily imagine where this saying came from. What if you actually had ants in your pants? You'd find it difficult to settle down. You'd keep squirming to get rid of the ants.

Apple of Your Eye

Kareem is the apple of my eye."

Meaning: a person or thing that is greatly loved, treasured, and adored

Origin: This saying is used in the Bible. Ancient people thought that the pupil of the eye was solid and shaped like an apple. The pupil ("apple of the eye") was precious because without it, you couldn't see.

As the Crow Flies

"Jennifer lives only a few blocks from school as the crow flies."

Meaning: by the shortest and most direct route; measured in a straight, direct line between two places

Origin: Most birds, including crows, fly to their destinations in a straight,

⇨

3

direct line. They don't zigzag or take detours. Therefore, they get where they're going by the most direct route. People can't always travel as directly as a crow flying through the air. They must walk, drive, or ride following the twists and turns. Measuring distances "as the crow flies" is often unrealistic because five miles between two points in a straight line might be ten miles of twists and turns, hills, and obstacles.

Asleep at the Switch

Shelley lost her job because she was asleep at the switch.

Meaning: not attending to one's job or failing to react quickly; not being alert

Origin: This saying comes from the early days of the railroad (the mid-1800s). One of a trainman's most important duties was to switch a train from one track to another at exactly the right moment. If he fell asleep at the switch, the train might go off the tracks or crash. Today the meaning has been extended to anyone who isn't paying attention and fails to do a job at the right time.

At the Drop of a Hat

"Olivia would have gone to the football game at the drop of a hat."

Meaning: right away; at once; without delay; willing at any moment

Origin: There are many ways to start a race or other sporting event: Shoot a gun, wave a flag, yell "Ready, set, go!" and so on. Years ago someone would drop a hat as the starting signal, and the contest would begin immediately. Today if anyone does anything (not just something athletic) eagerly and on the spur of the moment, we say it's done "at the drop of a hat."

At the End of Your Rope

"I've tried everything, but nothing's worked. I'm at the end of my rope."

Meaning: at the limit of your ability, endurance, or patience to do something

Origin: Imagine that you're trying to use rope to climb a mountain or a tree. You're at the end of your rope, and you can't achieve what you set out to do. Now just think of this expression in terms of any goal you are trying to accomplish, with or without an actual rope. You've run out of strength, power, or ideas on how to do more. Another possible origin of this saying is the fact that some farm animals are tied to a rope that will allow them to feed in a limited area, but not beyond.

Ax to Grind

Crystal always flatters me, but I think she has an **ax to grind**.

Meaning: something to gain for yourself for a selfish reason; flattery or trickery used to get a favor from another person

Origin: In the early 1800s a man wrote a story in a newspaper about how, when he was a boy, a man used flattery to trick him into sharpening the man's ax. The boy turned the heavy grindstone while the man held his ax against it because the man said the boy was a great ax grinder, smart and strong. The man didn't pay the boy or even thank him. Instead he scolded him for wasting time and being late for school. After that, people started using the expression "have an ax to grind" when they meant that anyone was seeking a particular goal solely for himself by flattering or tricking another person. Sometimes people say that they don't have an ax to grind to show that they are honest and aren't trying to trick you into doing anything for them.

Babe in the Woods

"Peter knew his way around junior high, but now in high school he's just a babe in the woods."

Meaning: a person who is inexperienced; a naive, trusting person

Origin: In 1595 a story called "The Children in the Wood" was published in England. It was about a greedy uncle who was supposed to be taking care of his rich niece and nephew. Instead, he hired two men to kill them so he could inherit their money. One of the men took pity on the children and left them in the woods rather than kill them. They did not survive. That's why we can say that inexperienced people or people that can't take care of themselves and can easily be misled or exploited are "babes in the woods."

Back to Square One

Our design for a solar-powered washing machine didn't work, so it's back to square one.

Meaning: return to the beginning because of a failure to accomplish the desired result

Origin: There are many board and street games that have squares or boxes. Each player must start at the first square and try to advance to the finish line or last box to win. If, for any reason, you have to go back to square one, you're starting over from the beginning. A similar saying is "back to the drawing board," where architects begin blueprints or sketches for each project. When a project fails to work out, you may have to start over again from the original drawings to improve your chances for success.

Backseat Driver

"I can fix this computer myself, but she always tries to be a backseat driver."

Meaning: a bossy person who tells another person what to do; a person who gives unwanted advice and directions

Origin: When automobiles became popular in the United States in the 1920s, many rich people rode around in the backseats of chauffeur-driven cars. The backseat passenger gave orders to the front-seat driver: where to go, what road to take, how fast to drive, and so on. Today "backseat driver" refers to any aggressive person, in or out of a car, who tries to tell others what to do.

Baker's Dozen

"At the garage sale, we charged 75¢ per baseball card or $9 for a baker's dozen."

Meaning: thirteen of anything for the price of twelve

Origin: A dozen of anything is twelve. Then why is a "baker's dozen" thirteen? Hundreds of years ago some English bakers cheated their customers by baking air pockets into loaves of bread, making them light-weight. In 1266 the English Parliament passed a law that said that bakers who sold underweight bread would be severely punished. To be sure they were selling enough bread to meet the new weight regulations, the bakers started giving thirteen loaves for every dozen a customer ordered.

Bark Is Worse than Your Bite

The new director yells a lot, but her bark is worse than her bite.

Meaning: the way a person sounds is much more frightening than the way she or he acts; the threat is often worse than the action taken

Origin: This expression was used as far back as the mid-1600s. A dog barking ferociously sounds like he could actually bite your head off. But if the dog does not hurt you, then his "bark is worse than his bite."

Bark Up the Wrong Tree

"Maria's uncle wanted to make her into a magician, but he was barking up the wrong tree. Her brother, Juan, was the one who loved tricks."

Meaning: to direct your attention or efforts toward the wrong person or thing; to have the wrong idea about something

Origin: During colonial times in America, raccoon hunting was a popular sport. Trained dogs would chase a raccoon up a tree and bark furiously at the base until the hunter came. Sometimes a raccoon could escape to the branches of another tree, leaving the dog barking up the wrong tree. Today, you can "bark up the wrong tree" if you're on a wrong course of action, have your attention redirected from your intended object, or choose the wrong person to deal with.

B

Batten Down the Hatches

We'd better batten down the hatches: The weather service says a tropical storm is headed our way.

Meaning: to get ready for trouble; prepare for any emergency

Origin: This is a nautical term that comes from the early 1800s. On a ship, sailors prepared for stormy weather by nailing waterproofed pieces of canvas and wood (battens) over the entryways (hatches) to the cargo area below the main deck. Today you "batten down the hatches" when you prepare for any kind of trouble.

Beat a Dead Horse

"He tried to convince his sister, but he was beating a dead horse."

Meaning: to pursue a useless goal; to continue fighting a battle which has been lost; to keep arguing a point which has already been decided

Origin: This saying goes back to the ancient Roman playwright Plautus who used it in 195 B.C. in one of his plays. The dramatic performance was of trying to whip a dead horse to get up and carry the load it was supposed to be moving. This action was shown to accomplish nothing. Today we say that anyone pursuing an issue that is already settled is "beating a dead horse."

Beat Around the Bush

"Stop beating around the bush. Whom are you taking to the dance?"

Meaning: to avoid answering a question; to approach something carefully or in a roundabout way

Origin: This expression goes all the way back to the 1500s when hunters hired people called beaters to drive small animals out of the bushes so the hunters could get a better shot at them. The problem for the beaters was that they might drive the birds or rabbits or foxes out too soon. They had to be careful not to drive the animals into the open before the hunters arrived. So the beaters might use their long sticks "around the bush" rather than directly on it. Today, the expression "to beat around the bush" means talking about things in a roundabout way without giving clear answers or coming to the point.

Beat the Band

When my sister told us that she was marrying Malcolm, everyone cheered to beat the band.

Meaning: with much noise, excitement, or commotion; very much, very fast; outdoing all others

Origin: This saying started in the late 1800s in Britain and then traveled across the Atlantic Ocean to the United States. One explanation of its origin is that since a band is usually loud, exciting, and colorful, anything that "beats the band" must be louder, more exciting, and more colorful. The other explanation is that people sometimes run ahead of a marching band to beat it to a certain spot. This idiom can also be used to express amazement for any astonishing achievement, as in "She can drive the tractor and she's only eight years old. If that doesn't beat the band!"

Beat Your Swords into Plowshares

"The prime minister would like them to beat their swords into plowshares and abandon all plans for war."

Meaning: to stop fighting and turn your attention toward peaceful activities

Origin: This is another of the many famous sayings that come from the Bible. In Isaiah 2:4 there appears the following sentence: "And they shall beat their swords into plowshares, and their spears into pruning hooks; nation shall not lift up sword against nation, neither shall they learn war any more." Swords and spears represent weapons of war. Plowshares and pruning hooks represent farming tools, which are symbols for all peaceful activities. So when a modern nation "beats its swords into plowshares," it could be manufacturing passenger planes instead of bombers, or VCRs instead of military radar systems.

Beauty Is in the Eye of the Beholder

"Lenny thinks his dog's haircut is cool. I guess beauty is in the eye of the beholder."

Meaning: there is no standard for beauty, so what one person likes or sees in someone or something is not necessarily what others see; different people have different opinions

⇨

Origin: Many writers in the past have stated the idea that what one person thinks is ugly, another person may think is beautiful. The "eye" is really the mind, thoughts, feelings, and emotions of the "beholder," or the person who is looking at the person or thing.

Bed of Roses

"Compared with my old school, this one is a bed of roses."

Meaning: a wonderful, pleasant situation or position; an easy, comfortable life

Origin: English poets have used this phrase for centuries. Roses are such lovely, sweet-smelling, soft-petaled flowers that a bed of them suggests a lovely, sweet, and soft condition. The meaning was stretched to mean any easy and comfortable situation in life. However, if you really think about it, roses have thorns and a real bed of roses would probably be anything but comfortable. A similar expression used today is "bowl of cherries."

Bee in Your Bonnet

Mr. Davis thinks he can teach us the trombone. He must have a bee in his bonnet.

Meaning: a crazy idea; an obsession with an idea

Origin: This 16th-century expression was originally "to have a head full of bees," but it changed to "bee in one's bonnet" in Robert Herrick's "Mad Maid's Song," a poem written in 1648. It sounds better this way because of alliteration—both words beginning with the same letter. If you have a crazy idea and can't talk about anything else, it's like having a bee stuck in your hat. A similar expression is to have "bats in your belfry."

Beggars Can't Be Choosers

"Beggars can't be choosers. If you don't have money to go out for pizza, you'll have to eat in the cafeteria."

Meaning: needy people have to take whatever they can get and cannot be concerned about the quality if they cannot afford to buy it for themselves

Origin: This proverb has been around since the mid-1500s. It means that people who need something but who have little or no control over their situations can't choose what they get. They have to accept what is offered.

Behind the Eight Ball

"My father caught me napping in the hammock instead of mowing the lawn. I'm really behind the eight ball now."

Meaning: in trouble or out of luck; in a difficult position or in a bad situation with little hope of winning

Origin: This American idiom from the early 1900s comes from billiards. In the game kellypool you have to hit numbered balls into pockets of a billiard table in numerical order, except for ball number eight, which is to be pocketed last. However, if the eight ball is very close to the ball you're trying to hit, you're in trouble. That's a bad position to be in. Today we say that anyone "behind the eight ball" is experiencing a lot of bad luck. Other similar idioms are "in a pretty kettle of fish," "up a creek," "in a pickle," "in the dog house," and "in hot water."

Bells and Whistles

"Our teacher says we're getting a new computer with all the latest bells and whistles: CD-ROM, modem, color printer, full multimedia."

Meaning: impressive accessories, especially flashy, high-technology features and frills, which may sometimes be more decorative than necessary

Origin: This modern phrase became popular with the development of many kinds of new electronic and computerized equipment. The "bells and whistles" represent all sorts of super high-tech features that you don't really need in a basic model but which make a product more fun to use (and more expensive). Note: "bells and whistles" don't have to make any sounds.

Better Half

I'm not making a decision until I check with my better half.

Meaning: either partner in marriage

Origin: Puritans were English Protestants in the 16th and 17th centuries who favored strict religious discipline. They said that each person was made up of two halves, body and soul, and that the soul was the better half because it was the spiritual side. Sir Philip Sidney, an English writer, said that a marriage was made up of two halves, and that the better half was the better spouse. Today when the phrase "better half" is used, it almost always means someone's wife, although there's no reason why a wife can't use the term to describe her husband. In either case, "better half" is a compliment.

Between a Rock and a Hard Place

"It's a tough choice between getting to the big game on time or waiting for Mr. Smith to call. I'm stuck between a rock and a hard place."

Meaning: being in a very tight spot and faced with a difficult decision

Origin: In this American saying from the early 20th century, you can picture someone actually squeezed between a rock and a hard place. He or she has to turn one way or the other, but neither way is very pleasant. A similar expression from an earlier time is "between the devil and the deep blue sea" (see next entry).

Between the Devil and the Deep Blue Sea

"Glenn had to choose between confessing that he hadn't studied or trying to fake it. He was between the devil and the deep blue sea."

Meaning: between two great dangers and not knowing what to do; in a very difficult position

Origin: In the early 17th century the heavy plank fastened to the side of a vessel as a support for guns was called the devil. Sometimes a sailor had to go out onto this plank to do repairs to the boat. In heavy seas he would be in great danger of falling overboard and drowning because he was between "the devil and the deep blue sea." Over the centuries the meaning of this expression expanded to include being between two equally difficult perils of any kind.

Beware of Greeks Bearing Gifts

Natasha is just giving you that CD because she wants one of your puppies. Beware of Greeks bearing gifts.

Meaning: be suspicious of presents from certain people who are just looking for something from you; be on guard against treachery in the disguise of a gift

Origin: The great ancient Roman writer Virgil used a similar sentence in his famous story of the Trojan War, the *Aeneid*. For ten years the Greek army tried in vain to conquer the city of Troy. Finally the Greeks pulled a rotten (but clever) trick on the Trojans. They pretended to sail back to Greece and left behind a huge wooden horse as a "gift." The Trojans brought the horse inside their city, but many Greek soldiers were hidden in the hollow belly of the horse. They came out at night, defeated the Trojans, and conquered the city.

Bird in the Hand Is Worth Two in the Bush

Take this job now because you don't know if you'll get the other one. Remember that a bird in the hand is worth two in the bush.

Meaning: what you already have is better than what you might or might not get in the future; a guarantee is worth more than a promise

Origin: This saying began as an ancient Greek proverb. Aesop used it in some of his fables. The ancient Romans repeated it, and in the 1400s it was translated into English. It comes from the sport of hunting birds. Hunters thought that a bird that you had already captured ("in the hand") was better than two you hadn't yet caught ("in the bush"). Today we often hear the same advice: It is better to be content with what you already have than to reject it because you hope that something better will turn up.

Birds of a Feather Flock Together

"Everyone at that table plays soccer. I guess that birds of a feather flock together."

Meaning: people who have things in common, such as interests and ideas, usually hang out together; people who are alike often become friends

Origin: This saying, which is over 2,000 years old and comes from the Bible, is based on the observation that birds of the same species flock together on the ground as well as in the air. The meaning has been broadened over the years, so that "birds" means "people" and "of a feather" means "of the same type."

13

Bite off More than You Can Chew

"You can't captain the team, edit the paper, and star in the play. Don't bite off more than you can chew."

Meaning: to take on a task that is more than you can accomplish; to be greedy, overconfident, or too ambitious by taking on more jobs or responsibilities than you can deal with at one time

Origin: Versions of this saying were used in Europe in the Middle Ages and ancient China. If you take a bite of food that's too big for your mouth, you won't be able to chew it. This idea came to mean undertaking ("biting off") a job that's too much for you to handle ("more than you can chew").

Bite the Bullet

The principal wants to see you in her office. Get ready to bite the bullet.

Meaning: prepare for an unpleasant experience; brace yourself to endure with courage something painful but necessary

Origin: Many word experts think that this expression came from the 19th century medical practice of giving a wounded soldier a bullet to bite before he was operated on without anesthetics on the battlefield. Biting on the soft lead bullet was the way of dealing with the pain. It kept the soldier from screaming, which could distract the surgeon during the operation.

Bite the Dust

"The spy bit the dust at the end of the book."

Meaning: to die; to fall in defeat; to fail to succeed

Origin: This cliché, which was often heard in early Western movies, is actually more than 2,000 years old and comes from a line in Homer's *Iliad*. It describes many dying warriors in the Trojan War falling to the earth and "biting the dust." If people fall with their faces in the dirt, you can think of them getting dust in their mouths. The idiom became popular in English in the mid-1800s

Bite the Hand that Feeds You

"Eve just insulted the girl who is teaching her to ice-skate. That's biting the hand that feeds you."

Meaning: to turn against someone who helps you; to do harm to someone who does good things for you

Origin: This saying, which has been used at least since the early 1700s, originally referred to a foolish and ungrateful dog that actually bit the hand of the owner who was feeding it. The meaning of this expression today has been extended to include people who turn against anyone who helps them. It has nothing to do with real food or actually biting anyone's hand.

Bite Your Tongue

"Don't you dare say that to me! Bite your tongue, young man!"

Meaning: take back or be ashamed of what you have said; struggle not to say something you want to say

Origin: It's easy to see where this saying came from. If you really put your tongue between your teeth as if you were biting it, you couldn't talk. So when people tell you to "bite your tongue," they are telling you to force yourself to be silent before you say something you shouldn't. Sometimes people say it after they've already blurted out what they shouldn't have. Then it means to take back the statement and keep quiet. A similar expression is "hold your tongue," which means you should remain silent.

Black Sheep of the Family

Geraldine's the black sheep of the family. She's always causing trouble.

Meaning: the most unsuccessful, least admirable member of a family or similar group; a disgraced person

Origin: This expression has been used at least since the early 1800s to describe a person who is a disgrace to a community or family. Shepherds did not like rare black sheep since their fleece could not be dyed any color and there weren't enough of them to sell black wool. Some people also thought that the black sheep frightened the rest of the flock and came from the devil. The saying changed over time to mean disfavored people in a family or group.

Bleeding Heart

"Rob is such a bleeding heart. He'll donate to any charity that asks him for money!"

Meaning: an extremely softhearted person who feels compassion or pity towards all people, including those who may not deserve sympathy

Origin: This controversial term comes from America in the 20th century. Some people say that government or private charities should do more to help relieve the suffering of the sick, the homeless, or the unemployed. These well-meaning citizens might be called "bleeding hearts" by others who feel that many people on welfare or charity should stop taking so much from others.

Blessing in Disguise

"Summer school may be a blessing in disguise. Next year you'll be ahead of your class."

Meaning: something that at first seems bad but turns out to be good; a hidden benefit

Origin: This saying was first used in a poem 200 years ago by a writer named James Hervey, and people have been using it since. When something looks like bad luck, it may turn out to be a false appearance (a "disguise") that hides something that's really useful or fortunate (a "blessing"). Of course, you don't know that at first because the blessing is in disguise.

Blind Leading the Blind

Kurt, who spent his allowance in one day, is showing Bonnie how to budget her money. That's a case of the blind leading the blind!

Meaning: the uninformed attempting to inform others

Origin: This saying comes from a sentence in the King James Bible (Matthew 15:14), "And if the blind lead the blind, both shall fall into the ditch." Today we use it to describe people who are not actually blind, but who don't know how to do something and are trying to explain it to other people who don't know how to do it either.

Blood Is Thicker than Water

"Mrs. Penn chose her grandson instead of me to work in her store. I guess blood is thicker than water."

Meaning: one can expect more kindness from a family member than from a stranger; a person will do more for a relative than for anyone else

Origin: This saying, that means that family ties count more than friendship, comes from Germany in the 12th century. Perhaps it comes from the idea that water can evaporate without leaving a trace, but blood leaves a stain and is more permanent. This suggests that relatives ("blood") are more important ("thicker") than people who are not related ("water").

Blow Your Own Horn

When you fill out an application for a job, blow your own horn.

Meaning: to praise yourself; to call attention to your own merits (intelligence, skills, success, or abilities); to brag about yourself

Origin: In ancient Roman times, a blare of trumpets announced the arrival of a great hero. So the blowing of horns meant someone important was coming. Today, people who blow (or toot) their own horns are boasting about their superior qualities. Sometimes you have to do that a little (when you apply for a job, for instance), but if you do it too much, you could be called a braggart.

Blue Blood

"Steve is marrying a very rich girl from high society, a real blue blood."

Meaning: of high or noble birth; an aristocrat; from the upper class of society

Origin: Though this expression has been used in English since the early 1800s, it actually comes from an older Spanish saying. Old, aristocratic Spanish families used to boast that their skin was fairly light because they had not intermarried with the darker-skinned Moors. The Spaniards' veins showed through their skins as visibly blue in color. If their skin was darker because they had intermarried, the blood would not appear so blue. "Blue blood" is a translation of the Spanish words *sangre azul*. Today anyone can be called a blue blood if he or she is of noble birth, a member of high society, and so on. A related phrase is "upper crust" (see page 201).

Bolt from the Blue

"Mr. Barnes's pop quiz hit us like a bolt from the blue."

Meaning: something sudden, unexpected, and shocking

Origin: This expression has been used since at least the early 1800s. Picture a calm, clear, blue sky. You'd probably be surprised, even startled, if a bolt of lightning suddenly cracked down. In the same way, any big surprise is like lightning shooting out of a clear, blue sky. You just don't expect it to happen. (Note: this expression usually refers to very bad news.) A related idiom is "out of the clear, blue sky" (see page 140).

Born with a Silver Spoon in Your Mouth

Fran always wants the finest, most expensive things. Was she born with a silver spoon in her mouth?

Meaning: born to wealth, comfort, and privilege

Origin: A spoon made out of pure silver is expensive. Sometimes a silver spoon is given as a gift to a newborn baby. If a rich baby has many expensive things from the start of life, like a silver spoon (almost as if he or she were born with the spoon in his or her mouth), we can use this well-known idiom to describe that person. The phrase was used by Cervantes, the Spanish writer, in the early 1600s in the book *Don Quixote*.

Bottom Line

"If we don't win this ball game, we're out of the playoffs. That's the bottom line."

Meaning: the most crucial fact; the net result

Origin: For hundreds of years accountants have added up the profits and losses of companies. The sum appears at the bottom line of a column of numbers. While "bottom line" still means a bookkeeping figure showing profit or loss, it has taken on a more general meaning since the mid-1900s, and now refers to any crucial decision or final result, financial or not.

Break a Leg

"On the night of the play, Holly's father told her to break a leg."

Meaning: good luck; do a great job in the show

Origin: Saying this to a performer before a show has long been a theatrical tradition. It comes from an old German saying, *Hals- und Beinbruch* (break your neck and leg), and was shortened to just the leg. Perhaps it exists because of an old show business superstition that wishing someone good luck might cause just the opposite to happen, so you wish the performer bad luck to assure the opposite of that.

Break the Ice

"Pierre was very shy when he met Cindy. He didn't know how to break the ice."

Meaning: to overcome the first awkward difficulties in a social situation by a friendly gesture; to ease the nervousness in a situation

Origin: As early as the late 1500s and early 1600s, writers like Shakespeare were using this expression. It originally came from navigation through waterways frozen over with ice. Special boats had to break through the ice, clearing the way before any ships could sail. The meaning was transferred to getting a conversation started or making an acquaintance. "Ice" in this idiom represents a cold or awkward feeling among people, especially strangers.

Bring Down the House

When our principal came out on stage dressed like a North High student, she brought down the house.

Meaning: to get an audience to clap enthusiastically or laugh loudly

Origin: This saying, which comes from the theater, has been in common use since the 1700s. Performers have long referred to the audience in a theater, and the theater itself, as the "house." When a performer is a huge success, and the excited audience is cheering, laughing, and applauding so wildly that the roof of the theater seems to be shaking and about to fall in, he or she has "brought down the house."

Bring Home the Bacon

> Both Richard and Samantha got jobs to bring home the bacon for their children.

Meaning: to support a family by working; to earn a living

Origin: There are two theories about where this expression came from. One was from the contest at early American county fairs of chasing after a greased pig. If you caught it, you could take it home as your prize. Another possibility is that it came from a practice in the early 1300s. A baron willed that if any married persons in Dunmow, England, swore at the church door that they had not had a single quarrel for a whole year and a day, they would get a free side of bacon to take home. The idiom "bring home the bacon" has, for hundreds of years, meant to score a point, win a game, or earn something of value, such as your salary.

Bug Off

"Helen told Max to bug off because he was being such a pest."

Meaning: to leave someone alone; go away; stop annoying someone

Origin: There was an expression in the late 1800s, "bugger off," that meant the same thing. Today's slightly shorter version is a rude slang expression, usually said by someone who is highly annoyed and wants the other person to leave him or her alone.

Bug Someone

"I wish you would just stop bugging me and leave me in peace!"

Meaning: to irritate, annoy, and bother someone a lot

Origin: This popular African-American idiom comes from the 1960s and is a handy expression when people are pestering you. It comes from *baga* and *bugal,* words in West African languages (Mandingo and Wolof) that mean "to annoy." By the way, in certain situations, "bug" can also mean to wiretap someone's phone so that his or her conversations can be listened in on.

Bull in a China Shop

"Inviting the wrestling team to the ceramics exhibit was like letting bulls into a china shop."

Meaning: a clumsy person who deals too roughly with a delicate situation; a rough person who is near breakable things; a tactless person who says or does something that angers people or upsets their plans

Origin: Aesop, the famous ancient storyteller, once wrote a fable about a donkey in a potter's shop. Aesop's image was changed to a bull in a china shop when fine plates and dishes, called china, were first introduced into Europe in the 1500s. (Why was "donkey" changed to "bull"? Probably because a bull is so much bigger.)

Burn the Candle at Both Ends

"Ms. Murphy goes to college during the day and works in a restaurant at night. She's burning the candle at both ends."

Meaning: to overwork yourself mentally or physically and until you're exhausted

Origin: This was a French expression that came into English in the late 1500s. If you really took a candle and burned it at both ends, it would be used up twice as fast. That image changed to refer to people who work hard night and day and use up all their strength. We also say that you can "burn yourself out" this way.

Burn the Midnight Oil

I have a big test tomorrow morning, so I plan to burn the midnight oil tonight.

Meaning: to stay up very late at night studying or working

Origin: This saying goes back to the days when lamps were lighted by oil and people went to bed earlier than they do today. When you burned the midnight oil in those days, you were up late working or reading by the light of an oil lamp.

Burn Your Bridges Behind You

"If you drop out of school now, you'll be burning your bridges behind you."

Meaning: to make a decision you cannot change; to commit oneself to a course of action

Origin: In ancient military history, soldiers actually burned down the bridge they had just crossed so they wouldn't be tempted to turn back in a cowardly way. (It also kept the enemy from following them over the same bridge.) Julius Caesar burned bridges to toughen up his troops.

Bury the Hatchet

Stop fighting, and bury the hatchet!

Meaning: to settle an argument; end a war; make peace; become friends after being enemies

Origin: This saying probably comes from American Indian tribes who would make peace with their enemies by holding a ceremony. They would actually bury tomahawks, hatchets, and other war weapons to show that the fight was over. If war broke out again, they would dig up the weapons. By the end of the 1800s the meaning of "bury the hatchet" was extended to include settling any kind of argument and making friends with your enemy.

Bury Your Head in the Sand

"You're burying your head in the sand if you think that smoking isn't bad for your health."

Meaning: to ignore danger by pretending you don't see it; to hide from obvious signs of danger

Origin: An ostrich is a big, tough bird, but long ago people got the wrong idea about it. Since they saw ostriches with their heads in the dirt, they thought the ostrich was hiding from its enemies in the false belief that if you can't see your enemy, your enemy can't see you. The ostriches were actually looking for seeds or berries on the ground, or eating bits of sand, which help the birds digest their food. Today "bury your head in the sand" has come to mean refusing to either notice a problem or face up to reality.

Busman's Holiday

Freddy went back to his carpentry shop after spending all weekend building our treehouse. What a busman's holiday!

Meaning: spending your free time doing the same thing you do during working hours

Origin: In London, during the late 1800s and early 1900s, buses were pulled by horses. Some bus drivers loved their horses so much that on their days off from work, they would ride on their own buses just to make sure that other bus drivers took good care of the horses. This habit got to be called a "busman's holiday," and today it can be applied to anybody who does the same thing on free time as he or she gets paid to do at work.

Busy as a Beaver

"Jeni is as busy as a beaver setting up her new computer."

Meaning: working very hard; extremely industrious

Origin: This saying comes from the 17th century. For hundreds of years the beaver has been a symbol of diligent work. Watch a beaver bustling about, busily cutting down trees with its teeth and energetically building a dam, and you'll easily see why. Alliteration (busy as a beaver) adds to the popularity of this simile. Related sayings: "busy as a bee" and "eager beaver."

Butter Someone Up

"Maybe if you butter up the math teacher, she'll raise your final grade."

Meaning: to flatter someone; to try to get a favor by praising someone

Origin: This saying comes from the simple act of buttering a slice of bread. When you take plain bread and lay on a thick coating of creamy butter, it's sort of like covering a person with praise and flattery. People often "butter" other people up when they want special help or favored treatment. Similar sayings: "to soft-soap" and "to sweet-talk."

Butterflies in the Stomach

"I can't sing a solo without getting butterflies in my stomach."

Meaning: a fluttery feeling in the stomach, usually caused by nervousness

Origin: If people are anxious, have stage fright, or are troubled about what will happen next, they often experience dull spasms in their stomachs. Some people call this sensation the flutters. Others say they have a nervous stomach. Once a clever writer imagined butterflies in his stomach when he felt panicky or uneasy, and that creative metaphor caught on.

Button Your Lip

"Renee talked about her vacation so much that we finally told her to button her lip."

Meaning: to stop talking; be quiet

Origin: It's easy to picture where this 20th-century American expression came from. Imagine buttons on people's lips. Someone who wanted you to stay quiet, keep a secret, and not say a word would tell you to button your lip. Today some people also use the expressions "button it up," "zipper your mouth," and "put a cork in it."

Buy a Pig in a Poke

Have the used car looked over by a mechanic before you pay for it. Don't buy a pig in a poke.

Meaning: to buy something without seeing or examining it

Origin: A long time ago in England, a small bag or sack was called a poke. Farmers carried their pigs in pokes to sell at markets and county fairs. Sometimes customers were cheated by dishonest farmers who had actually put a runt (an undersized pig) or even a cat in the sack. The farmer said he couldn't open the bag to show the customer the pig because it might run away. So if you bought a "pig in a poke," you paid for something without examining it. Today the expression applies to any kind of item you buy sight unseen. See also "let the cat out of the bag," (see page 111).

By Hook or by Crook

"Justin is grounded, but he'll find a way to get to my party by hook or by crook."

Meaning: by any means possible (legal or not)

Origin: Perhaps this idiom, which has been around at least since the 1300s, came from the idea that, as a last resort, you could get what you wanted by reaching it with a long hook or by stealing it like a crook. This expression owes some of its popularity to the fact that it rhymes.

By the Skin of Your Teeth

Aaron dove off the dock just as it collapsed and escaped injury by the skin of his teeth.

Meaning: by an extremely narrow margin; with practically no room to spare; just barely

Origin: This expression, which was first mentioned in the Bible, has been popular in English since about the beginning of the 1800s. Your teeth sometimes have a film on them, especially when you wake up in the morning. If you think of this film as "skin," then you can see that the "skin of your teeth" is thin indeed. If you avoid some terrible calamity by a margin of safety so small that it's as thin as the skin of your teeth, you've had an extremely close escape.

C

Call It a Day

You've been working on that history report since before breakfast. Why don't you **call it a day**?

Meaning: to stop work for the day; to bring a project to an end for the time being

Origin: The idea expressed in this idiom is that a certain amount of work is enough for one day. When you've done that amount, you should "call it a day," meaning to declare that you've done a full day's work and that you're stopping.

Call the Shots

"You may know all about glassblowing, but here in the gym, I **call the shots**."

Meaning: to make the decisions; to be in charge; to give orders

Origin: The origin of this expression is unclear, but it might refer to the officer in charge of soldiers in a battle. He gives the commands and calls the (gun) shots. The phrase also suggests the role of a coach of a basketball team who tells the players what plays to make and what (basketball) shots to take. Today we say that the person in charge of any kind of activity "calls the shots."

Call You on the Carpet

"My piano teacher **called me on the carpet** today. He could tell I hadn't practiced all week."

Meaning: to call a person before an authority for a scolding

Origin: There was an expression in Britain in the early 1800s, "to walk the carpet." That referred to a servant's being called into the parlor (which was always carpeted, unlike the servants' quarters) to be scolded by the master or mistress of the house. Later the saying was applied to an unlucky employe being called to the boss's office (also carpeted) to be bawled out. Today, if anyone in authority scolds you, you are being "called on the carpet" no matter how the floor is actually covered.

Call Your Bluff

> They're bragging they can beat us badly. C'mon. Let's call their bluff.

Meaning: to demand that someone prove a claim; to challenge someone to carry out a threat

Origin: This early 19th-century American saying comes from card playing. In poker, a player makes bets according to what his hand is, compared to what he thinks others' are. When you bluff, you pretend you have a great hand of cards even when you don't, and you raise the bet to fake out the other players. If someone "calls your bluff," he or she challenges you by meeting or raising your bet ("to call" means to match a bet) to make you show the cards you really have.

Calm Before the Storm

"The meeting may be peaceful now, but this is only the calm before the storm."

Meaning: a period of peace before a disturbance or crisis; an unnatural or false calm before a storm

Origin: There was an ancient Greek proverb that said "Fair weather brings on cloudy weather." Though that's not always true, people have noticed since the 1500s that there often was a period of stillness before a big storm. For over four centuries the meaning of this saying has been broadened to include any time of false peacefulness right before a violent outburst.

Can't Fight City Hall

"The school board is determined to make the school year longer. You can't fight city hall."

Meaning: an ordinary person cannot win a struggle against an administrative system

Origin: In the United States, "city hall" represents the local government: the mayor, the legislative body, as well as the various agencies and departments. Today when we say "city hall" we mean any large organization such as a government, school system, or corporation. This expression claims that you can't fight city hall, but that's not always true. You can protest, picket, circulate petitions, make speeches, write letters, support candidates who express your views, or even run for mayor yourself!

27

Can't Hit the Side of a Barn

"Don't worry about being the target in the booth at the school carnival. These kids can't hit the side of a barn."

Meaning: to have terrible aim; to not be able to throw well enough to hit even a large target

Origin: The side of a barn is a large area, and if you can't hit something as big as that, your pitching arm must be terrible. This idiom became popular in the United States in the early 1900s. It described baseball pitchers who couldn't throw the ball into the strike zone. Variations on this expression are "can't hit the broad side of a barn" and "can't hit a barn door."

Can't Hold a Candle To

Anita can't hold a candle to Jon when it comes to tap dancing.

Meaning: to be second-rate in a certain skill; to be greatly inferior

Origin: In the 1500s, long before the days of good lighting, a servant called a "link-boy" held candles for people. This was considered a lowly job done by those who were thought to be inferior. If a link-boy did not know the roads or the layout of a theater, then he was said to be "not worthy to hold a candle to someone." Thus, the expression "can't hold a candle to" came to mean lower in order, rank, quality, or value.

Can't See the Forest for the Trees

"My teacher catches all my grammar mistakes, but he misses my brilliant writing. He can't see the forest for the trees."

Meaning: to overlook the overall situation because of a focus on small details; to be so involved in details that you miss the whole picture

Origin: This idiom, which has been popular for many years, created this picture in the mind of the writer who invented it: a person in the country focuses so intently on each individual tree, leaf, branch, and twig, that she misses the splendor of the huge forest she's in. Afterwards, if someone asks her, "How did you like the forest?" she might answer, "What forest? All I saw were some trees." This saying means to be unable to understand the whole situation because you pay too much attention to the small parts.

Carry Coals to Newcastle

Taking flowers to the florist's daughter is like carrying coals to Newcastle.

Meaning: to do something unnecessary; to bring something to a place where it is already plentiful

Origin: There are many coal mines in the English city of Newcastle. Coal is shipped out from this port to other places. Newcastle definitely doesn't need extra coal, so if you carry coals there, you are doing something totally unnecessary. Today the meaning of this expression includes similar situations like taking snowballs to people living near the North Pole.

Carry the Ball

"As for organizing the ski trip, Angel will carry the ball."

Meaning: to be in charge or be responsible; to make sure that a job gets done right

Origin: This idiom comes from the world of sports, especially football. In many ball games, the most important person is the one who has the ball at the moment. This phrase expanded to include other areas of life, such as school, business, or government. The person holding the ball is the one responsible for the task.

Cast Pearls Before Swine

"Serving gourmet food to John is like casting pearls before swine. He likes fast food and jelly sandwiches."

Meaning: to waste something good or valuable on someone who won't appreciate or understand it

Origin: This expression comes from the Bible (Matthew 7:6) and was later used by famous writers such as William Shakespeare and Charles Dickens. Giving pearls to swine, or pigs, would be foolish. The pigs want mud and food, not precious jewels. In a similar way, wasting something good on someone who won't be thankful for it is like "casting pearls before swine."

Cast the First Stone

"Don't criticize. You've done it yourself, so you shouldn't cast the first stone."

Meaning: to be the first to attack, blame, or criticize someone; to lead accusers against a wrongdoer

Origin: This is another saying that comes from the Bible. The apostle John writes that when people wanted to stone to death a woman accused of something immoral, Jesus said, "He that is without sin among you, let him first cast a stone at her." In other words, you shouldn't criticize how others behave unless you're perfect yourself.

Cat Got Your Tongue?

Why don't you answer me? Cat got your tongue?

Meaning: Is there a reason that you're not speaking?

Origin: By the mid-1800s this expression was popular in both the United States and Britain. No one is sure where it came from, but you can imagine that if a cat really got hold of your tongue, you wouldn't be able to say a word. Probably someone thought up this saying to ask, "Why don't you talk?" in a clever way, and it caught on.

Catch More Flies with Honey than with Vinegar

"Ask her nicely. Remember, you can catch more flies with honey than with vinegar."

Meaning: more can be accomplished by being pleasant than by being disagreeable

Origin: As early as the 1600s people were using different versions of this expression in many European languages. If you've ever had a fly buzzing around your house, you know that it is attracted to sweet things like honey. It doesn't like sour things like vinegar. In the same way, you're more likely to get what you want from people ("catch more flies") by being sweet and agreeable (like honey), rather than bitter and sharp (like vinegar).

Catch Someone Red-Handed

"Ashley's brother was caught red-handed at the scene of the crime."

Meaning: to catch someone in the act of doing something wrong

Origin: At first this expression referred to someone caught in the middle of a murder with blood on his or her hands ("red-handed"). Later the saying grew to mean any kind of wrongdoing, not just a criminal action. If you were nabbed sneaking one of your grandmother's freshly baked brownies, for instance, your fingers might be covered with chocolate, but you'd still be caught "red-handed."

Catch You Later

I've got to get right home to baby-sit my sister. I'll catch you later.

Meaning: good-bye, I'll see or speak to you at another time

Origin: The verb "catch" has many meanings, including to capture, to trap, and to grasp or take hold of forcibly. In this late 20th century African-American expression, "catch" means to see or hear from you at a later time.

Champ at the Bit

"Steve couldn't wait to go into sixth grade. On the first day of school, he was champing at the bit at 6:00 A.M."

Meaning: to be impatient to start; to be ready and enthusiastic to do something

Origin: This saying, which has been used for at least 200 years, comes from horse racing. An eager racehorse champs, or bites, on the bit in its mouth at the start of a race. That shows that it is impatient with any delay and wants to be off and running. Today the meaning has been broadened to include not only horses at the starting gate but also anyone eager to start doing something.

Cheek by Jowl

"I thought that Omar and Mike had a fight, but I saw them today in the gym, cheek by jowl."

Meaning: very close together, side by side

Origin: William Shakespeare used a similar expression, "cheek by cheek," in his famous romantic comedy *A Midsummer Night's Dream,* written about 1595. "Cheek by jowl" was a variation invented two centuries later. "Jowl" is another word for the jaw or cheek. So if two people are together with one person's cheek right by another person's jowl, they're pretty close indeed.

Chew Someone Out

When Laurie's parents saw her report card, they really chewed her out.

Meaning: to scold severely or roughly; to bawl someone out

Origin: Did you ever watch someone's mouth and lips moving furiously when they were harshly scolding you? Perhaps it reminded a writer years ago of fast chewing, and that's how this expression was born.

Chew the Fat

"My friend and I sat up half the night just chewing the fat."

Meaning: to have a friendly, informal talk; to chat in a relaxed way

Origin: In the late 1800s this expression was popular in the British army, and then it came to the United States. One possible origin might be that military and naval people were given tough meat to eat and they had to chew the fat of the meat as they talked. The action of chewing is like the action of speaking (see "chew someone out"). At any rate, if you're just hanging out, talking with your friends in an easy, relaxed way, you're "chewing the fat" (or "rag"). A similar expression is to "shoot the breeze."

Chew Up the Scenery

"Josh was chewing up the scenery in the principal's office, crying and screaming that he didn't do it."

Meaning: to overact; to exaggerate your emotions

Origin: This idiom comes from show business. Some actors carry on wildly, and in exaggerated, overemotional ways. A critic once wrote that this kind of uncontrolled theatrical behavior was like chewing up the scenery, and the criticism soon became a popular phrase. Today people can "chew up the scenery" wherever they show too much emotion to achieve a special effect.

Chew Your Cud

"Don't bother your father right now. He's in the den chewing his cud over problems at work."

Meaning: to think deeply to oneself; to turn a matter over and over in your mind

Origin: In the mid-1500s a lot of people owned cows, sheep, and goats. These are animals that chew their cuds (food that is spit up from the stomach to the mouth and chewed again). It's a long process. A person lost in deep thought—pondering, reflecting, speculating—made a clever 16th-century writer think of an animal chewing its cud, and this saying was born. Sometimes it's shortened just to "chew over" a matter.

Chicken Feed

Mr. Baer loves his job at the museum, even though they pay only chicken feed.

Meaning: a very small or insignificant amount of money

Origin: This American barnyard saying came from the pioneer days. The grain for the chickens to eat had to be inexpensive. At one point in our country's history, "chicken feed" came to mean small coins. Today people use "chicken feed" when something costs only a little bit of money or they're getting low pay at work. "Chicken feed" sometimes means misleading information that is given to throw someone off the track.

Chickens Come Home to Roost

> You'd better be careful what you say when you're angry. Chickens come home to roost.

Meaning: words or actions come back to haunt a person; evil acts will return to plague the doer

Origin: In 1810 the English poet Robert South wrote, "Curses are like young chickens; they always come home to roost." If you live on a farm, you'll know that chickens allowed to run around the barnyard come back to the chicken coop to sleep. In this expression the "chickens" are angry words or thoughtless actions. When they "come home to roost," they come back to cause trouble. In other words, everyone has to deal with the results of his or her own actions.

Chill Out

"When Chris threw down the paddle after he lost the Ping-Pong game, the counselor told him to chill out."

Meaning: relax, calm down

Origin: When a person starts to get angry, we often use expressions like "steamed up" and "hot under the collar" to describe his or her emotions. If being heated up suggests being overly excited, then it's easy to see how the opposite means calm. "Chill out" is a recent African-American idiom, and so are other similar expressions like "take a chill pill" and "cool it."

Chip off the Old Block

"I never realized how much Felix looks like his father. He's a real chip off the old block."

Meaning: a child who resembles a parent in behavior, looks, or abilities.

Origin: This is an old expression. It's been popular for hundreds of years, and it may go back as far as the ancient Greeks. A "block" can be of wood or stone. If you chipped off a little piece of it, the chip would resemble the big block—for instance, in color and texture. In the same way, a child ("chip") might act or look like the parent ("the old block").

Chip on Your Shoulder

"Avoid Calvin today. He has a real chip on his shoulder."

Meaning: to be quarrelsome, aggressive, or rude; to be ready to fight

Origin: In the early 1800s American boys played the following game: One boy put a chip of wood or stone on his shoulder and dared another boy to knock it off. If he did, the two boys would fight. Today, if a person is edgy or looking for an argument, we say that he has a "chip on his shoulder," in reference to that old game.

Chips Are Down

"Girls, the chips are down. If we don't win this game, we're out of the playoffs."

Meaning: the situation is urgent and has to be dealt with now

Origin: This saying appeared in the United States in the 19th century and comes from gambling, probably poker. Chips are small plastic disks used like money for betting. A gambler puts his chips in front of him to show that he is willing to risk a certain amount of money on a bet. When his pile of chips is down (that is, his money is low), his situation is bad, maybe even desperate. Today the expression "chips are down" refers to any critical situation in life, such as in sports, business, or politics, and not just card playing.

Clam Up

When the boss asked who had left the copy machine on all night, Caitlin clammed up.

Meaning: to refuse to talk; to become silent

Origin: An imaginative writer once thought that a person's lips were like the two halves of a clamshell. When it wants to, a clam can shut its shell tightly. That's what gave that writer the idea to write "clam up" to mean "to shut your lips, and keep information to yourself." Other similar idioms are "button up," "button your lip," (see page 24), and "zip your lips."

(see page 24)

Clean as a Whistle

"The science lab is as clean as a whistle."

Meaning: completely free from dirt; perfectly neat

Origin: In one of his poems in the late 1700s, Robert Burns, a great Scottish poet, used a similar phrase, "as toom's a whissle" ("toom" meant "empty" then). The idea is that you can get the best, clearest, purest sound out of a whistle or any other wind instrument if you keep the reed (the part that makes the sound when you blow into it) completely free of dust and dirt. A similar expression is "clean as a hound's tooth."

Clean Bill of Health

The gas station that inspected Dad's old car gave it a clean bill of health.

Meaning: declaration of satisfactory, healthy condition, or proven innocence

Origin: In the 19th century people were often fearful that there might be diseases on ships that would dock in their cities. So health authorities had to inspect each ship before it could come near the wharf. If a ship was found to be free of disease, an official document called a "bill of health" was handed to the captain. Then the ship could dock. Today the expression refers to more than just medical health. If you've been accused of a crime, and then, after an investigation, were found not guilty, you're said to have been given "a clean bill of health."

Clear the Decks

"Before we can build our model for the science fair, we have to clear the decks of other homework."

Meaning: to get all of the minor details out of the way in order to focus on a major project

Origin: This is another of the many idioms that began at sea. In the times of wooden sailing ships, before the 1700s, crews got ready for a battle at sea by fastening down all loose objects on the cluttered deck that might get in the way or cause injuries. By the 18th century the expression had a broader meaning: deal with and get rid of all small matters that might stand in the way of getting a big job done.

Climb the Walls

The assembly was so dull that all the kids were climbing the walls.

Meaning: to be frustrated or anxious during a challenging situation; to be unable to endure

Origin: Perhaps this expression came from the days when soldiers attacking a castle climbed the walls of the stronghold. They wanted to get out of the situation they were in and get on with the battle. Today we say that any person can be "climbing the walls" when he or she feels the need for relief from a frustrating situation.

Clip Your Wings

"My father said that if I didn't start behaving, he was going to clip my wings."

Meaning: to end a person's privileges; to take away someone's power or freedom to do something

Origin: In ancient Rome thousands of years ago, people clipped the wings of pet birds so that they couldn't fly away. For centuries people have used the idiom "clip one's wings" to mean bringing a person under control.

Cloak-and-Dagger

"Dad reads books on gardening, while Mom loves a good cloak-and-dagger story."

Meaning: concerning or involving spies, secret agents, intrigue and mystery; involving plotting and scheming

Origin: As early as the 1600s theatergoers in Spain and other countries loved seeing melodramas filled with exciting adventures, especially daring sword fights. Many of the characters in these dramas hid daggers or swords under their cloaks. After a while, these shows were called "cloak-and-dagger" plays. Now the term is used to describe any kind of entertainment that involves espionage, suspense, or other dramatic adventures.

Close Shave

Roberto had a close shave. His coach almost caught him sneaking out of practice.

Meaning: a very narrow escape from danger

Origin: This American idiom comes from the early 19th century. The writer who coined this phrase saw the similarity between a close shave and a narrow escape from hazard. A close shave left your skin smooth, but if the blade came just a tiny bit closer, you'd be cut. Today, "close shave" implies a slender margin between safety and danger.

Cold Feet

"Jerry wanted to ask Lynette to the dance, but he got cold feet."

Meaning: a fear of doing something; a loss of nerve or confidence; second thoughts

Origin: Since the early 1800s people have been saying that someone who lost his courage had cold feet. Maybe it came from the idea of soldiers running away from battle. Fear can cause a person to feel quickly chilled, especially in the feet. Also, "hot" has always suggested eagerness to do something. A "hot-blooded" person, for instance, is always ready for a fight or an adventure. So, it's easy to see how "cold feet" can suggest cowardice and fear.

Cold Turkey

"I kicked the TV habit cold turkey. I took five books out of the library and covered my set with a blanket."

Meaning: the sudden stopping of any habit

Origin: This 20th-century American expression describes an instant withdrawal from any kind of habit, such as smoking, alcohol, drugs, or high-fat foods. If you totally quit your harmful behavior without any help, then you've quit "cold turkey." No one is quite sure why the words "cold" and "turkey" were joined this way. Since "cold" sometimes describes something unpleasant ("She gave me a cold stare," or "A cold chill ran down my spine," for example), then suddenly ending your bad, but pleasurable, habit could leave you cold. How the "turkey" gobbled its way into this idiom is anybody's guess.

Come Again

"He had a heavy accent, so when he told me his name, I had to say, 'Come again?'"

Meaning: I don't understand what you are saying, so please repeat yourself.

Origin: The verb "to come" has always meant to arrive or appear. In this 20th-century African-American expression, "come" takes on the meaning of "speak."

Come Apart at the Seams

"When Miriam found out that she wasn't going back to camp this summer, she came apart at the seams."

Meaning: to become so upset that all self-control is gone

Origin: A person doesn't actually have seams, of course, but think of a piece of clothing under great strain. Imagine a person trying to squeeze into a suit that was smaller than his or her size. The garment might come apart at the seams and rip open. Similarly, a nervous person under stress, could "come apart at the seams," or fall apart and break down.

Come Up Smelling like a Rose

Even though my sister forgot to do her chores last week, she still came up smelling like a rose.

Meaning: to get out of a possibly embarrassing or disgraceful situation without hurting your reputation, and maybe even improving it

Origin: This is a colorful 20th-century American expression. The writer who created it had in mind the image of a person who falls into a pile of garbage but manages to come up "smelling like a rose." Symbolically, this means the person gets into some kind of trouble, and through good fortune or cleverness, gets out again without damaging his or her good name.

Cook Your Goose

Loraine let the air out of Andrei's tires. That really cooked his goose.

Meaning: to put an end to; to ruin someone's plans

Origin: There is an old story about a medieval town under siege. The townspeople hung a goose from a tower as a symbol of stupidity meant to slight the enemy. But the gesture backfired when the attackers were so angered by the goose that they burned the whole town down, literally "cooking" the goose. Today, you "cook someone's goose" if you in any way spoil his or her plans or bring ruin.

Cooking with Gas

"Yesterday, he didn't score a single point. But in tonight's game, he was really cooking with gas."

Meaning: performing with skill, energy, enthusiasm, and excellence

Origin: Years ago when people wanted to cook food, they had to first gather wood and get a fire going. When gas cooking became popular in the 20th century, so did this African-American expression. Today, all you have to do is turn a dial. It's fast, clean, and effortless. The same idea can be applied to people's actions. When someone says you're "cooking with gas," he or she is complimenting you about whatever you're doing. You're getting the job done with great expertise and energy.

Cool as a Cucumber

"Roslyn was as cool as a cucumber when she got the award from the President of the United States."

Meaning: very calm; not nervous or emotional

Origin: As early as the 1500s this expression was used to describe calm and composed people. When thermometers were invented, scientists showed that cucumbers are often 20 degrees cooler inside than the outside air.

Cool It

I told Meryl and Micki to cool it and stop arguing.

Meaning: to relax, calm down; to stop being so excited or angry

Origin: This example of American slang, usually spoken as an irritated command, originated in the 1950s. When a person starts getting angry, a good piece of advice is to "cool it." Get control of yourself and relax.

Cool Your Heels

"Poor Jerry. I just saw him cooling his heels outside the principal's office."

Meaning: to be kept waiting for a long time, usually by someone in power or authority

Origin: Your feet become warm or hot when you run or walk. But when you are forced to sit for a long time or stand in one place, the heels of your feet stay cool. That's why, since the early 1600s, the saying is that when someone keeps you waiting, you're "cooling your heels."

Cost an Arm and a Leg

"It cost him an arm and a leg to go to Hawaii, but Mr. Wong really needed the vacation.

Meaning: very expensive; high-priced, though possibly not worth the cost

Origin: This popular mid-20th century American expression gets a lot of use as things get more expensive. Naturally, one's arms and legs are priceless, so what this saying implies is that if something is really expensive, then it's like paying for it with one of your limbs.

Crocodile Tears

"I begged and cried to go to the party, but Dad said I was crying crocodile tears."

Meaning: fake tears; false grief

Origin: Way back in ancient Rome (about A.D. 300), people were using this expression. About 1,000 years later, people enjoyed listening to a popular folktale about how crocodiles make loud weeping sounds to trap innocent prey who come close to see what all the wailing is about. The crocodiles supposedly weep fake tears even as they eat their victims. Later, British writers such as Shakespeare, Bacon, and Tennyson used "crocodile tears" to suggest insincere sympathy and pretended sorrow.

Cross that Bridge When You Come to It

How do you know they won't let you into the concert? Cross that bridge when you come to it.

Meaning: don't predict problems until they actually happen; don't worry about future events now; don't deal with a difficulty until you have to

Origin: This expression is old, and no one today is sure of exactly when or where it originated. However, it's easy to see the idea behind it. If a bridge is ten miles down the road, you can't worry now about whether it is dangerous to cross until you get there. In the same way, there's no sense worrying about something ahead of time. Wait until it happens and then deal with it.

Cry over Spilled Milk

"I'm sorry your wallet fell overboard, but there's no use crying over spilled milk."

Meaning: to cry or complain about an event that has already taken place and can't be changed

Origin: This famous saying was first used by writers in the mid-1600s and popularized by Canadian humorist Thomas Haliburton around 1836. The idea behind it is that if milk spills out of a container, you can't get it back in again, so you might as well not cry over it. Note: Sometimes you'll see "spilled" spelled as "spilt." That's because this is an old idiom and "spilt" is an old spelling.

Cry Wolf

"Don't worry if my little brother starts screaming that there's a ghost in his room. He always cries wolf."

Meaning: to give a false alarm of danger; to warn of a peril that you know is not real

Origin: One of Aesop's most famous fables tells of a bored shepherd boy who falsely cried that a wolf was killing his sheep. When people came and found out there was no wolf threatening the sheep, they were annoyed. The shepherd did this once too often; one day when a real wolf came, no one came when he called out, and the wolf ate the sheep.

Cut Off Your Nose to Spite Your Face

"Don't stay home because your ex-girlfriend is going to the dance with Juan. Why cut off your nose to spite your face?"

Meaning: to injure yourself out of anger toward another; to make a situation worse for yourself when angry with someone

Origin: Some people were using this proverb in Latin as early as 1200. There may have been a story about cutting off part of a long, ugly nose, only to succeed in disfiguring the whole face. Apply that same idea to any spiteful action you commit against another person that ends up harming only you.

Cut the Mustard

He was forty and many people thought he was too old to cut the mustard, but he hit over fifty homeruns.

Meaning: to be able to handle a job or fulfill the requirements

Origin: This is an example of late 19th-century American slang. "Mustard" meant the main attraction. If you could "cut the mustard," you could do something well. Why is it "cut" the mustard? Perhaps because mustard grows as a plant that has to be cut down, and if you can cut the mustard plant down, you must be a capable person. Another theory is that this expression comes from the military. There, "to pass muster" means to pass inspection, which may have changed over the years to "cut the mustard."

Cut Your Eyeteeth on Something

"Paula's been fooling around with cars since she was a kid. She cut her eyeteeth on them."

Meaning: to acquire wisdom; to gain valuable experience, often at a young age

Origin: When a baby's first teeth start growing in, the teeth are actually cutting through the gums. Children also chew on things in order to help new teeth break through the gum. Years ago the analogy of cutting teeth and having experiences early in life probably led a writer to create this expression. We think eyeteeth got their name because they are right under the eyes in the upper jaw. But no one knows why eyeteeth are mentioned in this expression since they're not the first teeth to grow in. Sometimes the saying is shortened to "cut your teeth" on something.

Cutting Edge

My brother works in nuclear physics. He's on the cutting edge of some pretty amazing discoveries.

Meaning: the forefront; the most advanced or important position, usually in science and technology

Origin: Scientific discoveries and technological advances throughout the 20th century have been incredible. Just as the cutting edge of a sharp knife makes contact before the rest of the knife when slicing through objects, a highly advanced discovery is said to be on the "cutting edge."

Dark-Horse Candidate

Everyone was surprised when Pedro won the election because he was a dark-horse candidate.

Meaning: a contestant about whom little is known and who wins unexpectedly

Origin: There are at least three possible origins to this idiom and all come from horse racing in the early 1800s. The first is that a dark horse was a fast runner whose speed was kept secret ("dark") until the race started, and who, to everyone's surprise, won. The second is that an owner of a fast horse sometimes dyed its hair black as a disguise before a big race. The third is that a certain American horse trader fooled people by disguising his fast black stallion as an ordinary saddle horse. He rode the horse into town, arranged for a race, took bets on it, and always won. The term was introduced into American politics with the surprise win of President James Polk in 1844.

Dead as a Doornail

"When Emily quit the show, the class play was as dead as a doornail."

Meaning: totally dead or hopeless; without a chance of success

Origin: A book in the mid-1300s first used this expression. Perhaps its origin was the image of a metal plate (called a doornail) being hit so many times by the door knocker that it had its life knocked out of it. Also, "dead as a doornail" contains alliteration, and so does this variation on the saying: "dead as a dodo" (an extinct bird). Either expression is a good way to describe something that is out of date or no longer in existence.

Dead Duck

"When Sam finds out that Laura spilled the goldfish bowl, she's a dead duck."

Meaning: a person who is ruined; a person or project unlikely to continue or survive

Origin: This expression dates from the mid- to late-1800s. "Dead" has often referred to an idea, plan, project, or person that is ruined, or hopeless. "Duck" added alliteration to help the saying become popular.

D

Dime a Dozen

Anthony thought his old Hardy Boys books were rare, but they were a dime a dozen.

Meaning: very common and inexpensive; easy to get and available anywhere

Origin: In 1786 the U.S. Continental Congress officially named the ten-cent coin a "dime." The dime soon became a popular coin. Millions were minted. Everyone had them. Since they were so cheap, so abundant, and so common the phrase "a dime a dozen" became a natural way to describe any everyday thing that was easy to get and of small value. And "dime" and "dozen" begin with the same letter, which makes the saying catchy through alliteration.

Do or Die

"Marcy was determined to win the gold medal, do or die!"

Meaning: to succeed or fail completely; to take the chance of ruining oneself in trying to succeed

Origin: "Do" means to achieve or get something done. "Die" doesn't necessarily mean that your life will end if you don't accomplish what you set out to. It is an exaggeration. If you make a do-or-die effort, you're trying your hardest to succeed, no matter what obstacles might be in the way.

Dog Days of Summer

Sales of air conditioners are usually highest during the dog days of summer."

Meaning: the hottest and most humid days of summer, usually much of July and August

Origin: In ancient Roman times people who studied astronomy knew that Sirius, the Dog Star, rose and set with the sun during the hottest weeks of the year, July through mid-August. People thought that the heat from the Dog Star combined with the heat from the sun to make those weeks extra hot. That's why people today call this uncomfortable time the "dog days." People tend to get bored and tired at this time because it's so hot outside.

Dog-Eat-Dog World

"When Anna got her first job, she realized what a dog-eat-dog world it was."

Meaning: a way of life marked by fierce competition in which people compete ruthlessly for survival or success

Origin: This saying might go back as far as the 1500s. Sometimes savage dogs who were desperately hungry would fight bitterly for the same piece of food. A writer who observed this created the expression "dog-eat-dog world" to describe the willingness of some people to fight and hurt others in a merciless competition to get what they wanted. Today this phrase is usually used to describe the worlds of business and politics.

Dog's Life

"Poor Mrs. Youngman. With that miserable job and those screaming children, she leads a dog's life."

Meaning: a bleak, harsh, terrible existence without much happiness or freedom

Origin: Erasmus, a Dutch scholar and theologian, used this expression in his writings around 1542. Today there is a great effort to treat dogs humanely, so many dogs lead good lives. But dogs generally don't live as well as people. In some countries dogs are not kept as pets, and, in fact, it is common to eat them. So this expression has come to mean leading a poor or unhappy life.

Don't Count Your Chickens Before They Hatch

I spent the money I planned to earn and then the job was canceled. I shouldn't have counted my chickens before they hatched.

Meaning: don't count on profits before you earn them or have them in hand

Origin: Aesop once wrote about a woman carrying a basket of eggs. In her mind she figured how much she would get for the chickens when the eggs hatched and exactly how she would spend the money. She got so excited, she dropped her egg basket. Every egg smashed. Today we use this fable to warn people not to be confident of getting a result, realizing an ambition, or making a profit before it actually happens.

Don't Look a Gift Horse in the Mouth

"When Sandy complained about her present, her dad told her not to look a gift horse in the mouth."

Meaning: don't complain if a gift is not perfect; take what you've been given without criticism or emphasis on its worth

Origin: You can tell how old a horse is by looking at the size and shape of its teeth. What "don't look a gift horse in the mouth" means is that if you find too many faults with a gift by examining it too closely, you're sure to be disappointed and possibly insult the person who gave it to you.

Don't Take any Wooden Nickels

"Have a good trip to Chicago, and don't take any wooden nickels."

Meaning: Don't let anyone cheat you or take advantage of you.

Origin: This popular American expression was first used in the early 1900s during the great migration from rural areas to the big cities. The phrase meant that one should beware of city slickers, people who would sometimes pass out counterfeit coins ("wooden nickels"). Soon wooden nickels came to represent any kind of trickery or double-dealing.

Dot Your I's and Cross Your T's

Mrs. Potter wants us to proofread our papers and dot all the i's and cross all the t's.

Meaning: to take great care over details

Origin: An expression similar to this first appeared in books in the early 1500s. If you want good penmanship, you'd better be careful with things like the dots over the i's and the lines crossing the t's. Today this widely used saying refers to being extremely thorough by paying close attention to details in whatever you do.

Down in the Dumps

"After she lost the election, Kim was down in the dumps."

Meaning: sad and depressed

Origin: You might think that "dumps" in this saying refers to a garbage dump, but it doesn't. Some word experts think that "dumps" comes from old German words that meant "mental haze," "dullness," or "gloomy." So, if you're in a mental fog because you're so unhappy, you're definitely "down in the dumps." Note the alliteration in this idiom. Similar, older expressions are "down in the mouth" and "down-at-the-heels."

Down the Drain

"When her company went out of business, her money went down the drain."

Meaning: lost forever; wasted

Origin: In some places, water is more precious than oil or gold. Without water, crops can't grow and people can't live. Once water goes down the drain, it's gone and cannot be retrieved. Today we say that anything precious that's been wasted or lost has gone "down the drain."

Down the Hatch

Grandma handed me a glass of smelly medicine and said, "Down the hatch."

Meaning: swallow a drink in one gulp

Origin: People have used this expression for centuries. A ship's passengers, crew, and cargo pass through an opening in the deck called the hatch. Sometime in the mid-1500s a clever toastmaker, probably a sailor, realized that a drink going into a person's mouth was like things going into the hatch of a ship. He lifted a glass to his lips and said, "Down the hatch," and a new toast was born.

Down-to-Earth

"Even though Rosie's parents are millionaires, they don't act snobbishly. They are really quite down-to-earth."

Meaning: practical; sensible; realistic

Origin: This expression dates from the first half of the 20th century. A person with his or her "head in the clouds" might be absentminded or full of daydreams. But a person who is "down-to-earth" is direct and practical. Earth is where useful things grow. It's where sensible people have their two feet firmly planted.

Down-to-the-Wire

I can't talk to you now. I'm **down-to-the-wire** on this research report.

Meaning: running out of time; at the very last minute

Origin: This saying started in the early 1900s and became popular by the 1940s. It comes from horse racing and the real or imaginary wire marking the end of the race. Today we refer to that finish line when we say that a person working until the last possible moment on a project is coming down-to-the-wire. Sometimes this expression can also describe a person who is very low on money.

Draw the Line At

"My parents give me a lot of freedom, but they **draw the line at** letting me stay out late on school nights."

Meaning: to set a specific limit, especially about behavior

Origin: For thousands of years, whenever land was being divided, a line was drawn to show the end of one person's property and the beginning of another person's. There might be trouble if people were not sure of the boundary lines. There are other possible origins from sports like cricket and tennis.

Dressed to the Nines

"When Ramon came into the gym on the night of the dance, he was **dressed to the nines.**"

Meaning: wearing fashionable clothing; dressed to attract attention

Origin: There are a number of theories about the word "nines" in this idiom that dates back at least to the 18th century. Two possibilities are that nine is a mystical or sacred number in numerology (3 x 3) and represents perfection. Another theory is that the saying comes from an Old English expression "dressed to then eyne" which meant dressed fashionably from your toes right up to the eyes ("to then eyne"). Over time the letter "n" shifted one space to the right and "eyne" became "neyne" and eventually "nines." The saying is sometimes expressed as "dressed to the teeth" or "dressed to kill." Kill means to impress someone, not to murder them.

Drive a Hard Bargain

"I had to trade him three of my best comic books for just one baseball card. He sure **drives a hard bargain**."

Meaning: to insist on hard terms in making an agreement that is often to your advantage; to buy or sell at a good price

Origin: This idiom goes back to Greek writings of A.D. 950. It made its way into English about 500 years later. To "drive" means to vigorously carry through some task; "hard" means tough.

Drive You Crazy

It **drives me crazy** if my little brother bangs on his drum when I'm on the phone.

Meaning: to make someone angry or confused; to make somebody very annoyed or frustrated

Origin: This popular expression originated in America in the 1900s. To "drive" has long meant to be in control of a situation (see "in the driver's seat" (see page 98) and "backseat driver" (see page 6). So if someone is doing something so annoying that it's making you lose your wits, then you're being driven "crazy, mad, nuts"—or even "up a wall."

Drop in the Bucket

"I've saved all month for a skateboard, but I still have only **a drop in the bucket**."

Meaning: a very small, insignificant amount

Origin: Sometimes this expression, which comes from the Bible (Isaiah 9:15), is "a drop in the ocean." It's easy to see that one little drop of water is close to nothing when compared with all the water in a bucket. In the same way, a small amount of anything is like a drop in the bucket when compared with the full amount that is needed or desired.

Drop You Like a Hot Potato

"When she found out that Mark was lying to her, she **dropped him like a hot potato**."

Meaning: to get rid of something or somebody as quickly as possible

Origin: A hot potato stays hot for a long time because it contains a lot of water. If someone actually handed you a hot potato, you'd drop it quickly. If you didn't, you'd burn your hand. A writer in the early 19th century used this simile to mean to abandon, or drop, someone or something as fast as possible. "Hot potato" by itself means any embarrassing or dangerous problem.

Dull as Dishwater

"Programs on that channel are as dull as dishwater."

Meaning: not inspiring; uninteresting

Origin: An earlier form of this English expression was "dull as ditchwater," meaning the muddy water of a ditch. Charles Dickens used it that way in a book in 1865 to describe something boring and tedious. Ditchwater is cloudy, and definitely not exciting. So is dishwater. The change in words probably occurred as a mispronunciation or a mistake in printing.

Dutch Treat

Peter and Tracy went Dutch treat to the movies.

Meaning: each person pays for his or her own food and entertainment

Origin: This expression came from American slang in the late 1800s. Some word experts think it was first used by people who observed the habits of Dutch immigrants, who were thrifty and saved their money. When people paid for their own food and entertainment, especially on a date, the practice was dubbed "Dutch treat." "Go Dutch" means the same thing.

Dyed-in-the-Wool

"Mr. Freedman is a dyed-in-the-wool Republican and has never voted for a Democrat in his life."

Meaning: complete, permanent; stubborn

Origin: If wool is dyed while still in its raw state, the dye lasts longer than wool dyed after being spun or woven. At least since 1579 the idea of something being so deeply a part of something else that it wouldn't be easily changed was applied to people who had strong, unchangeable beliefs with the expression "dyed-in-the-wool." This saying was first used in the political sense in 1830 during the administration of Andrew Jackson.

Early Bird Catches the Worm

"Sue slept overnight in front of the stadium in order to get concert tickets. The early bird catches the worm."

Meaning: a person who gets up early and starts a project ahead of others has the best chance of accomplishing his or her goal

Origin: Birds like to eat worms. If a bird arrives late where the worms are, it will probably go hungry. But the bird who gets there early is sure to get some food. In the 1600s the proverb "the early bird gets the worm" was written to show that human beings who don't delay in starting an undertaking will most likely get what they want.

Easy as Pie

I thought that getting my teacher to raise my grade would be as easy as pie.

Meaning: not difficult; requiring practically no effort

Origin: There are two similar modern idioms that mean extremely easy: "easy as pie" and "piece of cake." Why should they both relate to baked desserts? Perhaps to the people who coined the phrases, desserts were easier to make than other foods.

Easy as Rolling off a Log

"Doug told me that learning how to work the ceramics kiln was as easy as rolling off a log."

Meaning: very, very easy; requiring little or no effort

Origin: In the United States in the 1830s, when this idiom was first used, logs were often floated down rivers from the forests to the lumber mills. Men held contests to see who could stand upright on a floating log the longest. Most men fell into the river because it's extremely difficult to remain standing on a floating log and extremely easy to fall off one. So anything that's effortless is "as easy as rolling off a log." This expression is related to "easy as pie" (above).

Easy Come, Easy Go

"You spent all your birthday money in one morning? With you, it's easy come, easy go."

Meaning: something that is easily obtained, as money, can be lost or parted with just as easily

Origin: This saying goes all the way back to the famous *Canterbury Tales*, written in the 1300s. The author, Geoffrey Chaucer, was saying that if you get something quickly and easily without really working hard for it, you'll probably spend or lose it just as quickly.

Eat Crow

"I made Jon admit that he was wrong, and now he has to eat crow."

Meaning: to be forced to do something very disagreeable; to acknowledge a mistake or defeat

Origin: This is a saying from the War of 1812 when an American officer was forced to eat a dead crow. People who have actually eaten a crow say that it tastes horrible. To be forced to "eat crow" is humbling and humiliating, like having to admit that you've done or said something terribly wrong. It's a little like eating humble pie (below).

Eat Humble Pie

When he finds out how wrong he's been, he'll eat humble pie!

Meaning: to be apologetic or suffer humiliation; to act humble or admit guilt

Origin: This expression is very similar to "eat crow," but it comes from medieval times, when there really was a pie called an "umble" or "numble" pie. Umbles were the heart, liver, and entrails of deer and other animals, and only servants ate a pie made out of animals' guts. "Umble pie" was changed to "humble," which means lowly and meek. By the early 1800s the expression "eat humble pie" meant profusely apologizing for a humiliating error.

Eat Out of Your Hand

"That kid will be eating out of my hand when I show him my new video game."

Meaning: to be very cooperative and submissive; to believe and obey someone without question

Origin: This expression, from the 20th century, describes what a tame or trusting animal will do if you treat it right. The person who created this idiom applied the same idea to human beings who trust fully and obey without question. People don't actually eat out of anyone's hand, but they do behave like obedient animals sometimes.

Eat You Out of House and Home

"Matthew grew four inches, and he's eating his parents out of house and home."

Meaning: to be so expensive to feed and keep that the person paying cannot afford it

Origin: William Shakespeare used this famous saying in one of his plays around the year 1600, but it probably goes back as far as 2,000 years. "House" and "home" mean about the same thing, of course. Using them both in the one expression doubles the meaning.

Eat Your Hat

If we don't win this basketball game by at least twenty points, I'll eat my hat.

Meaning: a statement made when you are positive that something will happen

Origin: Many great writers, including Charles Dickens, have used this expression. The idea behind it is that you are 100 percent certain that some event will take place (or not take place). If the opposite of what you publicly predict unexpectedly happens, you will do something ridiculous like eat your hat. Since you expect your prediction to come true, you feel safe in promising that you'll do something stupid if it doesn't.

Eat Your Heart Out

After Elena lost the plane tickets, she ate her heart out over the mistake.

Meaning: to feel extremely unhappy about a hopeless situation; to make yourself sick with grief and worry

Origin: This expression goes all the way back to the ancient Greeks. The poet Homer used it in his famous epic poem the *Odyssey*. A person's heart has always been considered the center of his or her emotions. For instance, a person can be "brokenhearted," or have a "heart of gold." This idiom is saying that if you become thin and weak from sorrow, if your misery is making you sick, then it's as if you are figuratively eating your heart out. The expression can also mean to be extremely jealous. "When Marika got the lead in the school play, Fiona ate her heart out because she wanted it."

Eat Your Words

"He predicted that I'd fail biology, but I got a D. Now he'll have to eat his words."

Meaning: to have to take back what you said; to admit humbly that you were wrong

Origin: Words come out of your mouth. Food goes in to be eaten. If you've said something that turns out to be not true, maybe you wish you could take back those wrong words, put them back into your mouth, and eat them. A similar expression is "eat crow" (see page 54), but "eat your words" makes more sense.

Egg on Your Face

"When Doug found out he had scored a touchdown for the other team, he had egg on his face."

Meaning: to be very embarrassed or humiliated for something foolish that you did or said

Origin: This American saying is probably from the 1950s. It could have come from the image of a sloppy eater, humiliated because he or she has food, like egg, on his or her face. Or it could have come from the custom of rude audiences in the old days throwing raw eggs at performers they didn't like. To be standing on a stage in front of an angry crowd with egg on your face must have been mortifying.

Elbow Grease

"Put a little elbow grease into that job. Polish that car until it shines!"

Meaning: hard, energetic manual labor

Origin: In Britain in the late 1600s people were using the term "elbow grease" to jokingly refer to the sweat worked up by strong, fast-moving work with one's arms, such as rubbing, polishing, and scraping.

Eleventh Hour

"At the eleventh hour, just seconds before the curtain rose, Sybil finished painting the scenery."

Meaning: at the latest possible time, just before the absolute deadline

Origin: This idiom comes from the Bible. The eleventh hour is the last hour before the end of the world. In the Bible, it was the last hour of sunlight with the twelfth hour bringing darkness. Some people delay so much, they sometimes finish a project at the last minute, or even the last second, just before the deadline passes.

Every Cloud Has a Silver Lining

"Nancy missed the school bus, but every cloud has a silver lining. She also missed the math test."

Meaning: there is something good in every bad situation

Origin: This expression of hope was used by the English poet John Milton in 1634. He must have noticed that if the sun is behind a dark cloud, light shines out around the edges like a silver lining. With this idiom, Milton said that even the worst situation ("cloud") has something hopeful or more positive about it ("silver lining").

Every Tom, Dick, and Harry

I wanted this to be a small, private party, but Victoria invited every Tom, Dick, and Harry.

Meaning: every person possible, especially very ordinary people

Origin: William Shakespeare used a phrase like this in one of his plays around 1600, but the last of the three names he used was Francis. In the early 1800s a lot of men were named Harry; that name replaced Francis and joined Tom and Dick, also common names, to stand for anybody and everybody, including ordinary people of low social status. "Tom, Dick, and Harry" is a put-down, usually spoken by a person who thinks that he or she is better than other people.

Everything but the Kitchen Sink

When Erin went away to college, she took everything but the kitchen sink.

Meaning: practically everything there is; every possible object whether needed or not

Origin: This expression was born in the early 20th century and became popular after World War II (the late 1940s). The kitchen sink is heavy, connected to pipes, and usually bolted down, so it's not easily movable. But if you took everything but the kitchen sink, you'd be taking virtually all there was. Related sayings are "from soup to nuts" (see page 69) and "from A to Z."

Eye for an Eye and a Tooth for a Tooth

"Amanda took Mac's bicycle after he took her skateboard. That's what I call an eye for an eye and a tooth for a tooth."

Meaning: revenge or punishment exactly like the original crime or offense

Origin: This idea appears in the Old Testament of the Bible (Exodus 21:23) and is often used to sum up its stern code. This idiom suggests that every crime or injury should be punished or paid back with an equal exchange of hurtful actions.

Eyes in the Back of Your Head

"My teacher always knows when we're passing notes. He must have eyes in the back of his head."

Meaning: ability to sense what is happening outside one's field of vision; ability to know what happens when one's back is turned

Origin: People's eyes are on the front of their faces, but there are people who seem to know what's going on behind them, as if they had eyes in the back of their heads.

Face the Music

I was caught cheating and now I have to face the music.

Meaning: to endure the consequences of one's actions; to take what you have coming to you

Origin: This American saying was common in the mid-1800s. There are two theories about its origin. It could have come from the world of theater. Sometimes an audience didn't like a show. It took courage for a performer to stand on the stage and face the hostile audience and also the orchestra pit ("the music"). This idiom could also have come from the military world. If a soldier did something dishonorable, he was often dismissed from the army as the band played, "facing the music." Similar expressions are "pay the piper" and "take one's medicine."

Fair-Weather Friend

"You can't count on Liz to help you when you're in trouble. She's just a fair-weather friend."

Meaning: a person who is a faithful friend only when everything is going well but who deserts you in time of difficulty

Origin: It's good when the weather is fair and lovely, with blue skies and mild breezes. It's bad when the weather turns foul. Apply the same idea to a friendship and you can see where this idiom came from. A fair-weather (good-time only) friend is the opposite of a friend in need (time of trouble).

Famous Last Words

"Our music teacher said that we were sure to win the state choral championship—famous last words."

Meaning: a sarcastic response to a foolish statement that suggests that the speaker doesn't know what he or she is talking about

Origin: It is thought that people in the military made this phrase popular during World War II (in the 1940s) and that other people began using it after that. Throughout history, people have made declarations ("This is the war to end all wars") that were later proven to be untrue and perhaps even silly to have been said in the first place. Simple-minded statements were sometimes referred to as "famous last words of history." The phrase was shortened to "famous last words."

Fat Cat

"Maybe we can get some fat cats to contribute money for the new gym."

Meaning: a wealthy person; a rich benefactor

Origin: This term, which goes back to the 1920s in America, used to refer to rich people who gave big contributions to political candidates. "Fat" described both the size of their waistlines (because they could afford big meals) and the size of their wallets (stuffed with money). Where did "cat" come from? It rhymes with "fat," and rhyming sounds often help a saying become popular.

Feast or Famine

"Last week we made over $100 on our car wash; this week only one car came. It's either feast or famine."

Meaning: great success or total failure; either too much or too little of something

Origin: This catchy phrase suggests the opposites of having too much or too little of something. "Feast" and "famine" are antonyms (words with opposite meanings) and also begin with the same sound (alliteration). This expression started out as "feast or fast" in the 1730s, but later "fast" was changed to "famine," which means about the same thing but doesn't sound as good with "feast." Why the switch of words? Nobody today really knows.

Feather in Your Cap

Winning the competition was quite a feather in my cap.

Meaning: a great achievement or special honor; an accomplishment to be proud of

Origin: It has been a custom of many different groups of people all over the world, including American Indians, to put a feather in the headgear of a warrior for each enemy defeated in battle. The more feathers in your cap, the greater your number of victories. Although the practice goes back to medieval times, the expression "feather in your cap" dates from just the early 17th century.

Feather Your Nest

"The senator was accused of using his office to feather his own nest."

Meaning: to be more interested in taking care of yourself, providing for your own comfort, and making money rather than doing good for others

Origin: For millions of years birds have been lining their nests with soft feathers to make comfortable homes. Since the 1500s the expression "feather your nest" has been used to refer to greedy people who use the power of high positions to make life comfortable for themselves before they think of the well-being of others. The saying can also be used in a more positive way to mean decorating your home to make it more pleasant and comfortable.

Feel Your Oats

Ms. Blumenthal was dancing, laughing, and feeling her oats.

Meaning: to be in high spirits, energetic; to act in a proud way

Origin: This American expression from the early 19th century originated when a writer noticed that his horse always acted more lively and vigorous when it was well-fed with oats. The writer applied the idea to people, often older ones, and wrote that a peppy, active person was "feeling his oats."

Feet of Clay

"In American history we learned that many Presidents had feet of clay."

Meaning: a hidden fault of character; a weak point

Origin: In the Bible (Daniel 2:31-32), the king of a great empire once dreamed of a statue with a head of gold, a body of silver and brass, legs of iron, and feet of iron and clay. The statue broke and its pieces blew away in the wind. The king's prophet interpreted the dream to mean that the empire would eventually break up. Even today, people who are highly regarded may have secret flaws of character ("feet of clay") that could ruin their reputations.

F

Fiddle While Rome Burns

The governor fiddled while Rome burned, doing nothing about crime, poverty, and pollution.

Meaning: do nothing or busy yourself with unimportant matters instead of taking action in an urgent situation

Origin: There's a famous legend that in A.D. 64 the emperor Nero stood on a high tower and played his lyre ("fiddle") while he watched Rome burn. The story may not be true, but it yielded this idiom that describes the behavior of anyone who, in a crisis, doesn't take action right away.

Field Day

"Andrew has a field day playing with all the new toys in his uncle's store."

Meaning: to have unlimited opportunities; to have it all your own way; to go all out and experience success at something

Origin: In the 1800s people from schools, fire companies, businesses, and other organizations would participate in wholesome outdoor sports on a big playing field. They would play to their heart's content. Soon, to have a field day meant to indulge yourself in any way you wanted. Even today, some schools have a "field day."

Fifth Wheel

"If he comes with us, he'll just be a fifth wheel."

Meaning: an unneeded, extra person

Origin: This is a proverb that was first used in France in the 16th century. A unicycle has one wheel; a bicycle has two wheels; a tricycle has three wheels; and wagons and cars have four wheels. No vehicle needs five wheels. The fifth wheel is a surplus thing, good for nothing. In the same way, if two couples are going out on a double date, an extra person who tags along could be called a "fifth wheel."

Fight Tooth and Nail

> The counselor had to separate two campers who were fighting tooth and nail.

Meaning: to fight fiercely, furiously, and ferociously

Origin: This vivid expression goes far back to a Latin proverb that became a French saying centuries later and finally came into English in 1562. When wild animals fight, they bite and claw each other. Sometimes people fight fiercely, as if they were animals fighting a deadly battle "tooth and nail."

Fill the Bill

"The decorator said that a tall potted palm in this corner would fill the bill."

Meaning: to be just the perfect thing that is needed; to be very competent, effective

Origin: One of the many meanings of "bill" is a list of acts being presented in a theater. In the 1800s an audience expected to enjoy a full bill of singers, dancers, jugglers, and comedians. To be sure that the audience was satisfied with the evening's lineup, the theater manager sometimes added acts to "fill the bill." Today the meaning has broadened to anything or anyone that meets a need or is just right for a purpose.

Finger in Every Pie

"Mrs. Simon has her finger in every pie when it comes to music, dance, and theater."

Meaning: to have a part in something; to be involved in many matters, businesses, or activities

Origin: The image that possibly created this expression might be of a person who can't decide what pie he or she wants—blueberry, pecan, peach—so they stick a finger in every pie to get a taste of each. Think of each pie as a different business or project, and when you put your finger into a "pie," you have a part interest or responsibility in that activity. People often participate in many activities to make extra profit for themselves.

Fish or Cut Bait

"Are you using that microscope or not? Fish or cut bait."

Meaning: do one thing or another, but stop delaying; make a choice; act now or give someone else a turn

Origin: This idiom, popular since the 1800s, is a metaphor that refers to a person who holds a fishing rod but doesn't fish. Someone else could use that rod and catch some fish. The procrastinator might be asked to either drop the line into the water and fish, or cut the bait from the line and let another angler have a chance.

Fish Out of Water

I want to help the new girl from Russia. She must feel like a fish out of water.

Meaning: a person who is out of his or her usual place; someone who doesn't fit in or is helpless in a situation

Origin: For thousands of years people have known that a fish belongs in water. That's its natural habitat. So a person who is in an unfamiliar or uncomfortable setting will feel like a fish out of water.

Fit as a Fiddle

"My great-grandfather is nearly ninety, but he's still fit as a fiddle."

Meaning: in good health; in fine shape

Origin: This expression dates from at least the early 1600s. "Fit" has always meant "in good health." But why was it joined with "fiddle" in this simile? Probably because "fit" and "fiddle" are a good example of alliteration, and a fiddle that's fit (well tuned and in good shape) can play terrific music.

Fix Your Wagon

"Maya borrowed my homework sheet and then left it at home. I'll fix her wagon."

Meaning: to get even with or to punish someone; to thwart or frustrate another or cause his or her failure in something

Origin: Some people think this idiom may have come from the days of the great westward migration in America in the 1800s, when the covered wagon was the main means of transportation. One meaning of the word "fix" is to take revenge upon or get even with. It might also mean tying up and holding secure, as in tying up a wagon so it cannot roll away. Today, "fix someone's wagon" means to plot against that person to do something bad to him or her.

Flash in the Pan

"People thought she was going to be a great concert violinist, but Dana was just a flash in the pan."

Meaning: a temporary success which yields no long-term results; a person who fails to live up to earlier potential

Origin: In the 1600s there was a popular gun called a flintlock musket. When the trigger was pulled, sparks were supposed to make the gunpowder in a small pan on the gun go off and explode the main charge. But sometimes there was only a flash in the pan and no big explosion. Today a "flash in the pan" is any person who showed great early promise ("sparks") but who never lived up to his or her full potential ("explosion").

Flotsam and Jetsam

I'm clearing out my room of all the flotsam and jetsam.

Meaning: a collection of mostly worthless and useless objects; odds and ends; any objects found floating or washed ashore; rubbish and refuse

Origin: The words "flotsam" and "jetsam" date from the early 1500s. Flotsam means all the wreckage and cargo floating in the ocean after a shipwreck. Jetsam is cargo and equipment floating in the water that was thrown overboard to lighten a ship in danger of sinking. By the 19th century these words meant any kind of junk or debris on land or sea, thrown out or not. The near-rhyming sound of the words helped make this idiom popular.

Fly-by-Night

"The store where I bought that defective CD player was a fly-by-night operation."

Meaning: selling for quick profit then disappearing; a swindler or unreliable person

Origin: Fly-by-night was an ancient term that described a woman who was thought to be like a witch. Witches were supposed to fly at night on brooms, and the term came to mean anyone who flies hurriedly from an activity. In the late 1800s this expression was made up to describe a person or business that sneaked away in the middle of the night to avoid paying bills or making good on promises to customers.

Fly by the Seat of Your Pants

"I had to entertain Dad's friends from Italy. I didn't know their language, so I just flew by the seat of my pants."

Meaning: to do something by instinct and feel without any earlier experience or instruction

Origin: This phrase was popular among members of the U.S. Army Air Corps in the 1930s. Often, there were few or no instruments on the planes and sometimes the instruments didn't work. So a pilot had to sit tight (on the seat of his pants) and fly an airplane by instinct. Today if you're doing any kind of project and there are no instructions, you may have to "fly by the seat of your pants." You proceed by intuition, natural talent, or common sense.

Fly in the Ointment

The food, the music, and the decorations were perfect, but her camera broke. That was the fly in the ointment.

Meaning: a small annoyance that spoils an otherwise pleasant situation

Origin: This saying comes from the Bible (Ecclesiastes 10:1). Thousands of years ago, people realized that a tiny nuisance can sometimes ruin something pleasant. Ointment is a creamy substance that soothes, softens, or heals the skin. Finding a fly in the ointment would certainly ruin it.

Fly off the Handle

"When Dr. Anthony discovered that someone had sneaked a look at the report cards, he really flew off the handle."

Meaning: to lose your temper; to become furiously angry

Origin: Many Americans in the early 1800s used handmade tools with axheads to chop down trees and build houses. The tools were often crudely made and the axhead would fly off the handle during furious chopping. The flying axhead is much like an angry person out of control.

Fly the Coop

I tucked my little brother into bed, but the next time I looked, he had flown the coop.

Meaning: to escape; to leave suddenly and secretly

Origin: A coop is an enclosure or cage for poultry or small animals. If a chicken "flew the coop," it escaped its pen. In the late 1800s and early 1900s "coop" was also a slang word for jail, so this expression often referred to what an escaped prisoner did. Today it is used in connection with any person or animal that secretly escapes or runs away.

Foam at the Mouth

"Dad was foaming at the mouth when he found out that Jerry had slipped out of the house."

Meaning: to be uncontrollably furious, like a mad dog

Origin: A dog with rabies or distemper foams at the mouth. A bubbly saliva forms around the lips, and the dog behaves in a crazy manner. As long ago as the 1400s people began describing furious people as "foaming at the mouth," as if they were mad dogs.

Follow Your Nose

"When he asked me the way to the cafeteria, I told him to follow his nose."

Meaning: to go straight ahead in the same direction

Origin: This saying was being used as early as the 15th century, maybe even earlier. Your nose is in the middle of your face, pointing straight ahead of you. So, if you "follow your nose," you proceed directly ahead. This saying usually has nothing to do with the nose's ability to smell things. However, someone directing you to the school cafeteria, a perfume factory, or a skunk farm might also tell you to "follow your nose," even if you have to take three lefts and a right.

Food for Thought

"The sign said, 'If all else fails, read the instructions.' That was food for thought."

Meaning: an interesting idea worth thinking about carefully

Origin: People have used this metaphorical saying since the early 1800s. In it, we think of the mind as a mouth that "chews" not food, but ideas. So ideas are the "food for thought." We sometimes use a related idiom, "to chew over an idea," which means to think about it seriously.

Footloose and Fancy-Free

"He doesn't have a girlfriend right now. He's just footloose and fancy-free."

Meaning: not attached to anyone; not involved with anyone romantically; free

Origin: In the 16th century, "fancy" meant love and "fancy-free" meant that you weren't in love with anyone. In the late 17th century, "footloose" meant you were free to go anywhere. (Your foot was "loose," not tied to something.) Today the expression means you're not bound to any one place, job, or person.

For the Birds

That movie was for the birds. I'm sorry I wasted my money on it.

Meaning: worthless; useless; stupid

Origin: This American slang was popular among soldiers during the first half of the 1900s. Think of bits of food left on the ground after a picnic. They're not worth anything, except, of course, to birds looking for crumbs. In the same way, we say that anything or anyone bad or silly is "for the birds."

Forty Winks

"I just need forty winks and I'll be able to work all night."

Meaning: a short nap

Origin: Since the 1300s, "wink" has referred to sleep, but probably just a short period of sleep because when you wink you close and open your eyelids quickly. In the Bible and the works of William Shakespeare, the number forty didn't always mean the number after thirty-nine. It meant an indefinite number or "few." The phrase "forty winks" was first used in 1872 in an issue of the famous British humor magazine *Punch*.

Four Corners of the Earth

"When John F. Kennedy died, people came to his funeral from the four corners of the earth."

Meaning: from all over the planet; all parts of a place

Origin: This saying first appeared in the New Testament of the Bible. Some ancient peoples thought that the planet Earth was flat and had corners. So when they referred to the "four corners of the earth," they meant some place near the edge of a rectangular map, the farthest ends of the world.

From Soup to Nuts

We've got acts in this talent show from soup to nuts: jugglers, acrobats, singers, magicians, tap dancers, you name it!

Meaning: the whole thing from beginning to end

Origin: For centuries any foods served at the beginning or end of a meal stood for the entire thing: the start and finish and everything in between. This expression was "from eggs to apples" and "from pottage to cheese." In the United States, in the middle of the 20th century, the expression developed into "from soup to nuts." At many meals, soup is often the first course and a dessert with nuts is sometimes the last. The expression does not have to refer only to meals, however. It could be the selection of goods for sale or classes offered.

From the Word Go

"Her mother did not like her boyfriend from the word go."

Meaning: from the very beginning

Origin: At the start of many races, someone shouts, "Ready, set, GO!" So, since the mid-1800s in the United States, "from the word go" has meant from the outset of something.

Full of Beans

"After final exams, some of us were exhausted and others were full of beans."

Meaning: lively, happy and energetic, high-spirited

Origin: Just as the expression to "feel your oats" means to be lively and frisky, being "full of beans" is a similar food-related idiom. Eating lots of beans has a gastrointestinal effect on some people that may make them a little more lively. The origin may also be from the days when the race-horses were fed beans. This lively expression has been bouncing around since the 1800s.

Full of Hot Air

I don't believe a word he says. He's full of hot air.

Meaning: being foolish and talking nonsense; pompous; vain

Origin: When you talk, warm air comes out of your mouth. Large balloons that carry people in baskets are kept afloat by hot air. This idiom from the mid-1800s puts those two ideas together. If you want to describe a pompous person who is all puffed up (like a balloon), you could say he or she is "full of hot air" (that's coming out of his or her mouth).

Get a Handle on Something

Rachel had a lot of trouble with geometry, but I think she's getting a handle on it.

Meaning: to find a way to understand or deal with something; to start to overcome a difficult problem or situation

Origin: This bit of American slang became popular in the mid-1900s. Did you ever try to lift up a heavy, bulky object that had no handles? How do you get a secure grip on it? The answer is to attach a handle to it. Today this expression refers to any difficulty you need to deal with or get control of. When you finally "get a handle on it," you start to solve the problem.

Get a Kick Out of Something

"My grandmother really gets a kick out of playing these video games with me."

Meaning: to enjoy doing something; to get a thrill out of something

Origin: A famous songwriter, Cole Porter, made this 20th-century American saying popular in his 1934 song "I Get a Kick Out of You." The title means "I really enjoy being with you." In this expression "kick" has to do with a thrill, not striking something with your foot. There are two variations on this idiom: "get a bang out of something" and "get a charge out of something." All three words—kick, bang, charge—suggest something that will really shake you up.

Get Away With Murder

"It's a darling cocker spaniel, but they let it get away with murder."

Meaning: to do something bad, wrong, or illegal and not get caught or punished

Origin: This American expression from the late 20th century is really an exaggeration. It can refer to any offense, major or minor, that you're not punished for, such as chewing gum in class, cheating on a test, or stealing. But, figuratively speaking, if you can get away without being punished for murder, you can probably get away with less serious crimes.

Get Down to Brass Tacks

"Let's get down to brass tacks. How much does this computer cost?"

Meaning: to go straight to the basic facts of the matter; begin the most important work or business; to get started with the essentials

Origin: Although this idiom has been widely used since the early 1900s, word experts are not sure what "brass tacks" stand for. The phrase might refer to copper bolts on a boat that have been scrubbed clean, or to brass-topped tacks used in the upholstery trade. If you get down to business by discussing the most basic, essential, and practical realities, then you're "getting down to brass tacks."

Get in on the Ground Floor

"Miss Cohen got in on the ground floor with a new women's clothing company."

Meaning: to be part of some big or important project or business at its start

Origin: This saying probably originated in the financial world of the late 1800s. It's an advantage to get in at the beginning of an enterprise. As the company succeeds and prospers, so will you. After all, you were there at the start and helped it grow. The ground floor is where you enter a big building. After that, there's no place to go but up.

Get into the Swing of Things

Anna didn't join in many activities at first, but now she's gotten into the swing of things.

Meaning: to become accustomed to routine activities

Origin: In the 1500s the phrase, "in full swing," meant to be very active in something. "Swing" could have come from the motion of a children's swing or a clock pendulum. In the 1800s a new expression developed that was based on the old one: "get into the swing of things." That meant getting involved with whatever was going on, especially socially.

Get off the Hook

"I don't want to baby-sit tonight, so I hope my sister will get me off the hook."

Meaning: to free yourself or someone from a distasteful obligation; to get out of trouble; to evade a punishment

Origin: This expression comes from fishing. If a fish is caught on a hook, it desperately wants to be off the hook. In the same way, if people are in trouble, have unwanted obligations, or are about to be punished, they want to "get off the hook" by ridding themselves of all these burdens.

Get Out of My Face

You'd better get out of my face right now or you'll be sorry!

Meaning: stop standing in front of me in a provocative manner, close to my face, arguing with me, or disapproving of my actions

Origin: This recent, vivid African-American expression means exactly what it says. Stop facing me in a way that causes trouble between us. Get away! Leave me alone! It is usually said in anger and with the understanding that if the other person doesn't stop talking and move away fast, he or she will suffer consequences.

Get Real

"Mrs. Gonzales isn't going to believe that weird excuse you gave her. Get real."

Meaning: face reality; think and act in a serious fashion; stop fantasizing

Origin: In just two words, this strong, modern African-American expression is an order to give up illusions and white lies. Stop pretending and confront the real world.

Get Something off Your Chest

"Something is bothering me, and I want to get it off my chest. Please don't smoke here."

Meaning: to make known something that is bothersome, angering, or irritating, but kept secret for a time

⇨

Origin: Your heart is in your chest, and the heart "feels" emotions such as love and fear. So if some worry, criticism, or secret has been troubling you and you finally tell someone, you're getting it "off your chest" (out of your heart) at last.

Get the Lead Out of Your Feet

C'mon, you guys. Get moving. Get the lead out of your feet!

Meaning: to get busy; to move or work more quickly

Origin: This expression, which was used a lot in the American armed forces during the Second World War, suggested that if you were moving sluggishly or working slowly, it was as if you had lead, a heavy metal, in your feet. If you got it out, you could speed up your actions. Another version of this idiom is "Get the lead out of your pants."

Get the Sack

"I had a great job at Heavenly Hamburgers, but the boss gave me the sack."

Meaning: to be fired

Origin: There are many expressions that mean to be dismissed from work, including "get the ax," "get a pink slip," and "get your walking papers." "Get the sack" might go back as far as the 1500s. In those days workmen who traveled around from job to job carried all their tools in a sack. If a man was fired, he was told to get his sack, pack up his tools, and move on.

Get to the Bottom of Something

"The principal vowed to get to the bottom of the graffiti on the walls."

Meaning: to find out the real cause of something; to uncover the hidden reason for something

Origin: Writers were using this expression in the late 1500s. The bottom is usually the base or root. If you search and investigate enough, you'll get to the bottom of something. Then you'll know how it got started.

Get Under Your Skin

"It really gets under my skin when my parents clean up my room."

Meaning: to bother or upset someone

Origin: If something irritating like a bug gets under your skin, it can cause a bad rash and itching. In the same way, if a person does something that irritates or upsets you, he's "getting under your skin." The famous American songwriter Cole Porter put a different twist on this expression when he wrote "I've Got You Under My Skin" in 1936. He changed the expression to suggest romantic addiction instead of annoying irritation.

Get-Up-and-Go

Since Grandmother joined that health club, she's had a lot more get-up-and-go.

Meaning: energy and motivation; pep; enthusiasm; ambition

Origin: This early 20th-century American expression means just what it says: get up and go rather than sit still and do nothing. It probably started as a verb phrase ("I wish she would get up and go") and eventually turned into a noun ("She needs more get-up-and-go").

Get Up on the Wrong Side of the Bed

"Watch out! Mother got up on the wrong side of the bed."

Meaning: to awake with a bad temper or mood, feeling cross or grouchy

Origin: In the time of the ancient Romans the left side of anything was considered evil or menacing. In fact, the word "sinister" comes from the Latin word for "left." The ancient Romans thought bad luck would come to anyone who put his or her left foot down first when getting out of bed. The expression began as "got up left foot forward." The superstition that left was bad continued for centuries and gave birth to today's expression "get up on the wrong side of the bed."

75

Get Your Feet Wet

"Grace had never been in a play, but she took a small part just to get her feet wet."

Meaning: to have a first experience in something; to begin to do something for the first time

Origin: This expression has been used for centuries, as far back as the 1500s. Imagine a swimmer who is afraid of diving into the water. He tiptoes in slowly, just getting his feet wet so he can get used to the water. Then he can plunge in when he's ready. In the same way, we "get our feet wet" when we venture into new territory by having our first experience with something.

Get Your Goat

"It really got my uncle's goat when he cooked for three hours and no one ate the meal."

Meaning: to annoy very badly; to make a person angry

Origin: This American expression dates from about 1900. It was a common practice to put a goat in the stall of a nervous racehorse to be its friend and keep it calm. If people wanted the horse to lose a race, they would sneak the goat out of the stall to upset the horse. There are several expressions that also mean to disturb or annoy someone: "get your dander up," "get your back up," and "get your hackles up."

Gift of Gab

Uncle Frank really had the gift of gab.

Meaning: skill in talking, especially in an interesting and colorful way

Origin: As early as the late 1600s and early 1700s, British writers and speakers were using this phrase. There are a few theories about its origin. Middle Dutch was a language used from the middle of the 12th century through the 15th, and the word for foolish chatter was "gabbelen." In the Gaelic language (spoken by some people in Scotland and Ireland) the word for mouth is "gob," and over the years it may have changed to "gab," the English word that today means to talk a lot about small matters. So today, somehow, between "gabbelen" and "gob," we get the "gift of gab."

Gild the Lily

She really doesn't need all that makeup. That's like gilding the lily.

Meaning: to spoil something that is already beautiful by adding something extra or not needed

Origin: William Shakespeare used a similar expression in his play *King John*: "to gild refined gold, to paint the lily...is wasteful and ridiculous excess." Over the years the saying got shortened to just "gild the lily." "Gild" means to cover with a thin layer of gold. Why did Shakespeare use "lily"? Because it is already a beautiful flower, and covering it with gold to make it more beautiful would be unnecessary.

Give Me Five

"My little cousin always yells, 'Give me five!'"

Meaning: to slap a person's hand as a hearty greeting or a sign of solid agreement

Origin: "Five" in this 20th-century African-American expression refers to fingers on your hand. Giving someone your five fingers (and your palm, too) is a common gesture when meeting. (A similar saying is "give me some skin.") This way of saying hello, showing harmony, or celebrating victory comes from a style of communication used in West Africa.

Give Someone the Shirt off Your Back

"Mr. Perez would give you the shirt off of his back if you needed it."

Meaning: to be extremely generous

Origin: First used in the 1770s, this idiom is almost self-explanatory. If you saw a needy person in the street who was cold because he had no shirt, and you actually took your own shirt off and gave it to him, it would be an act of great kindness. Today, if you perform any act of self-sacrifice, we say it's like "giving the shirt off your back to someone."

Give Up the Ghost

"On the way to the theater, Ernesto's old car just gave up the ghost."

Meaning: to die; to stop running

Origin: This saying started in the Bible (Job 14:10). "Ghost" in this idiom doesn't mean a dead person. It means the soul, which is thought to leave the body when a person dies. So if somebody "gives up the ghost," he or she stops living; if something "gives up the ghost," it stops working.

Give Your Eyeteeth for Something

"I'd give my eyeteeth to own a motorcycle like that."

Meaning: to want something very badly; to be willing to give up something valuable to get something else

Origin: Some people think eyeteeth got their name in the 1500s because the nerves of these teeth are close to the eyes. Eyeteeth are important because they're used for biting and chewing. If you want something so much that you are willing to sacrifice your eyeteeth for it, that thing must be extremely important to you. A similar expression is "to give your right arm" for something.

Go Against the Grain

It really goes against the grain when Nikolai says that a woman wouldn't make a good class president.

Meaning: to oppose natural tendencies; to oppose a person's wishes or feelings; to cause anger

Origin: This is another phrase that William Shakespeare popularized in one of his plays. The grain of a piece of wood is the direction of growth of the tree from which the wood came. If you were to saw that wood "against the grain" (across, rather than in the direction of, the wood fibers), it would be hard work. In the same way, anything that someone does or says that goes against the grain would definitely annoy or trouble you. To use another popular expression, it would "rub you the wrong way" (see page 165).

Go Along for the Ride

"Harriet swore that she didn't trash any lawns. She just went along for the ride."

Meaning: to watch but not take part in an activity; to keep someone company

Origin: This idiom was born in the late 1890s, at the beginning of the automobile age. Originally, it meant exactly what it said. If you had nothing better to do, you might go along with people for a ride in their car. The driver was doing something (driving the car) for a purpose (to get somewhere). You weren't doing anything, just sitting there in the car, looking out the window. Today we say that you're "going along for the ride" if you're joining an activity just to have something to do or just to be with other people.

Go Bananas

Come quick! Your brother has gone bananas.

Meaning: to be or go crazy

Origin: This saying comes from 20th-century America. Bananas are the food most associated with monkeys. When people think of monkeys ("monkey business," "more fun than a barrelful of monkeys," etc.) they think of silly, uncontrolled behavior. If a person is in a weird mood because he or she feels frustrated or bored with a situation, he or she might "go bananas" and start acting like a monkey.

Go Fly a Kite

"When he asked for her help, she told him to go fly a kite."

Meaning: go away; leave; stop bothering me

Origin: Imagine you're trying to do homework, and someone is really annoying you. There are a lot of expressions that you could shout at him that are similar to "Go fly a kite!": "Go jump in the lake!" "Go climb a tree!" "Go fry an egg!" You're telling the kid that he is a pest, and you're commanding him to go away and do something else. Flying a kite is an activity that should keep him busy so that you can get your work done.

79

Go for Broke

> Instead of applying to several colleges, he went for broke and applied only to his first choice.

Meaning: to risk everything on one big goal or effort; to try as hard as possible

Origin: Since the 17th century "broke" has meant "without money." Two hundred years later, this idiom was created at the gambling tables. When a gambler "went for broke," he risked all his money at once in a wager. If he won, he was rich. If he lost, he was broke. Today, people who "go for broke" try as hard as possible to achieve a single goal.

Go over Like a Lead Balloon

"I asked to go to Antarctica for vacation, but my idea went over like a lead balloon."

Meaning: to fail miserably

Origin: This is a fairly recent expression. The writer who first used it imagined what would happen if you tried to float a balloon filled with lead. It would never get off the ground. In the same way, any project or attempt that fails miserably is like a lead balloon that doesn't go over a blade of grass, let alone a treetop. This expression is often applied to a joke that gets no laughs.

Go over with a Fine-Tooth Comb

"She went over the lawn with a fine-tooth comb, but she couldn't find her contact lens."

Meaning: to search with great care or attention

Origin: A fine-tooth comb has teeth spaced very closely together. It is often used to help find and comb lice, which are very tiny, out of people's hair. Figuratively speaking, if you search an area with a fine-tooth comb, you're examining and inspecting it with great care so you won't miss a thing, no matter how small. A related idiom is "leave no stone unturned" (see page 109).

Go to the Dogs

"He used to be a handsome movie star, but now he's gone to the dogs."

Meaning: to decline in looks or health; to be ruined or destroyed; to ruin oneself

Origin: As far back as the 1500s, food that was not thought suitable for human consumption was thrown to the dogs. The expression caught on and expanded to include any person or thing that came to a bad end, was ruined, or looked terrible. For a similar phrase, see "gone to pot" (below).

Gone to Pot

This was once a beautiful park, but now it's all gone to pot.

Meaning: become ruined; to get worse and worse

Origin: This idiom from the 1500s originally referred to old or weak animals that couldn't breed, lay eggs, give milk, or pull wagons. They were more useful on the dinner plate than in the barnyard, so they were slaughtered and cooked in a pot. Now we describe anyone or anything as having "gone to pot" if the person or thing has worn out, is in bad shape, or can't do its job properly. Other similar expressions are "go to wrack and ruin" and "go to the dogs."

Goody-Two-Shoes

"Tamika is such a goody-two-shoes that everyone hates her."

Meaning: a person who thinks he or she is perfect and tries to be

Origin: In the middle 1700s there was a nursery tale called "The History of Little Good Two-Shoes." In it, a little girl who owned only one shoe was given another one. She went all over, showing off her pair of shoes, saying, "Two shoes." Today, a person who thinks he or she is perfect is sarcastically described as a "goody-two-shoes," after the title character of that book. A similar phrase is "goody-goody."

81

Grasp at Straws

"I guessed at half the answers on the biology test. I was just grasping at straws."

Meaning: to depend on something useless in a time of trouble; to make a hopeless effort to save yourself; to try something with little hope of succeeding

Origin: Ancient people made up this expression. They thought of a drowning person. He clutched frantically at reeds (hollow, strawlike grass) that grew on the banks of the river in a desperate, futile attempt to save himself. By the 1600s "clutching (or grasping) at straws" had become a popular proverb to express the idea of depending on something useless to help when there is trouble or danger.

Gravy Train

The kid was already asleep when he went to baby-sit. What a gravy train.

Meaning: a job that pays well for little work

Origin: This bit of American slang originated in the 1920s, when "gravy" was a slang word for easy money often gotten by illegal means. People who worked on railroad trains made up the phrase "gravy train." It referred to a good-paying job that was easy.

Greek to Me

"The computer saleswoman explained how to install the CD-ROM, but it was Greek to me."

Meaning: too difficult to understand; unknown

Origin: William Shakespeare used this phrase in one of his plays, *Julius Caesar*. In the play, which takes places in 44 B.C., a Roman who spoke only Latin said that he had heard another man speaking Greek, but he could not understand what he was saying. It was "Greek to him." The expression caught on. Today, if you don't understand something you've heard or read because it is so complicated or technical, then it's "Greek to you."

Green Thumb

"My uncle has a green thumb. You should see his roses."

Meaning: having a special talent for making flowers and green plants grow well

Origin: If you rubbed green plant leaves or parts between your fingers, you'd probably get chlorophyll, the green pigment of plants, on them. If a person loves gardening and has great ability to make plants grow, it's easy to see why people would say that he or she has a "green thumb."

Green with Envy

"When Sun Lee sees my new roller blades, he'll be green with envy."

Meaning: extremely jealous

Origin: Colors often take on descriptive meanings. Red sometimes means angry. Blue describes sad and lonely feelings. And since about 1600, thanks to William Shakespeare, green has been associated with jealousy and desire. He referred to jealousy as "the green sickness" in his play *Antony and Cleopatra*.

Grit Your Teeth

I have to remove this splinter from your finger, so just grit your teeth.

Meaning: to not show one's feelings; to put up with a difficulty; to bear pain courageously

Origin: In 18th-century America this expression was becoming popular. The ancient Greeks had used a similar expression that translated as "set your teeth." One of the definitions of the verb "grit" is to clamp your teeth together tightly. When people are faced with a tough or painful job that demands a lot of physical or emotional strength, they may grit their teeth in determination. Related sayings are "bite the bullet" (see page 14) and "face the music" (see page 59).

Gum Up the Works

I had set the VCR when my little cousin shot his water pistol at it and gummed up the works.

Meaning: to cause a machine or a system to break down; make something go wrong or throw it into confusion

Origin: This expression was first used in the 1800s, when a lot of new machines were being invented. Most machinery had to be oiled well to work properly. Sometimes the oil got so thick and gummy that, instead of helping the machine run smoothly, it actually interfered with—or even stopped—the working of the machine. Today, anyone or anything that "gums up the works" ruins someone's plans or spoils any kind of undertaking.

Handle with Kid Gloves

When you're speaking to Courtney, handle the subject of summer vacation with kid gloves.

Meaning: to treat gently and carefully

Origin: Kid gloves are made from the smooth hide of a young goat and are gentle to the touch. If you handle anything (like a fragile sculpture) or anyone (like your grumpy uncle) "with kid gloves," you're being careful and gentle. The last thing you want to do is break the sculpture or anger your uncle. You're making every attempt to avoid all possible problems.

Hand-to-Mouth Existence

"He lives a hand-to-mouth existence doing odd jobs around town."

Meaning: to spend your salary as fast as it's earned without saving any for the future

Origin: Writers were using this saying in the 16th century. Imagine a starving person who is given food. If he could, he'd save some for later, but because he's so hungry, he gobbles it all down. Every morsel goes directly from his hands into his mouth. Today we say that a person lives a "hand-to-mouth" existence (or "from hand to mouth") when he or she lives from day to day, spending every dollar earned without being able to put aside any savings for the future.

Handwriting on the Wall

"When the police questioned him, Phil saw the handwriting on the wall and confessed."

Meaning: a sign that something bad is going to happen; a warning of danger or trouble

Origin: This idiom originated in the Old Testament of the Bible. The King of Babylonia had a vision in which he saw a mysterious message written on the palace wall, *"Mene, mene, tekel, upharsin."* Daniel was sent for to explain the meaning of the strange words. When he arrived, he told the king that it was a warning that his kingdom would be conquered. In time the prophecy came true. Today we say that you can read or see the "handwriting on the wall" when you can see signs that misfortune is coming.

Hang in There

My brother kept calling, "Hang in there, you can do it!" And I did!

Meaning: to continue without giving up; to not lose faith or courage

Origin: This American slang expression probably came from boxing. A fighter who's exhausted but doesn't want to give up might hang on the arms of his opponent or on the ropes around the ring. That way he'll stop getting punched and be able to rest for a few seconds so he can get himself back up and continue the fight. By using this expression, you don't actually have to be hanging on to something physical in order to make it through a tough situation or a difficult project.

Hang Out Your Shingle

"After many years of training, she hung out her shingle, 'Nilda Sanchez, Animal Doctor.'"

Meaning: to open a private office, especially a doctor's or lawyer's office, by putting up a sign over the door

Origin: In 19th-century America, when professional people opened private offices, they hung out signs that were often painted on a shingle, a thin piece of wood used to cover the roof or sides of a building. Today we use the phrase "hang out your shingle" to refer to the whole process of opening up your own office: renting the space, filling it with furniture, hiring help, and hanging up the sign that announces you're in business.

Hanging by a Thread

"You are not quite failing, but you are hanging by a thread."

Meaning: to be in a dangerous or unsafe position; to depend on something very small to save you

Origin: There's a myth that tells of a king in the 5th century B.C. who grew tired of being told how wonderful he was by a flatterer named Damocles. The king threw a magnificent banquet for Damocles, who was having a grand time until he looked at the ceiling. He was shocked to see a large, sharp sword hanging by a single, thin hair, and pointing straight down at his head! He quickly learned his lesson: Power and happiness are not secure, and usually depend on the will or favor of someone else. Today, when people are in risky situations, we say they're "hanging by a thread."

Hard Nut to Crack

"That last algebra problem was a hard nut to crack."

Meaning: a problem that's very difficult to understand or solve; a difficult person

Origin: Benjamin Franklin used this expression, which had been popular since the early 1700s. In those days people didn't buy nuts that had already been cracked out of their shells. They had to do the cracking by hand, and some nuts were tough to crack. Later, the meaning came to include any kind of complicated jam or even a person who was hard to persuade.

Hat in Hand

Hat in hand, I went to the judge pleading for mercy.

Meaning: to behave in a humble and sorry way; to beg or plead for a favor or a pardon

Origin: For centuries people have begged for money in public by holding out a container to passersby. Often it was a hat. Taking off your hat in the presence of others is an act of respect. So a person, even one without a hat, who is begging for favors or forgiveness is a person with his or her "hat in hand." A related saying is "pass the hat" (see page 143).

Have a Bone to Pick with You

"My new boss said she had a bone to pick with me and called me into her office."

Meaning: to have an argument or unpleasant matter to settle with someone

Origin: This saying goes back to the early 16th century, and is based on the image of people arguing over fine points like dogs picking over bones to get every last bit of meat. Others think it may have originated in the 19th century from the idea that two people can argue the way two dogs can fight over a bone. In either case, if someone has "a bone to pick" with you, it means he or she has a complaint about something you said or did.

Have a Screw Loose

"That substitute gym teacher must have had a screw loose."

Meaning: to behave or look in a strange or foolish manner; to be odd and not ordinary

Origin: During the machine age beginning around 1860, many contraptions were held together by nuts, bolts, and screws. If a screw came loose, the machine would not operate as it was supposed to. It might start to do all sorts of bizarre things. People aren't held together with screws, of course, but if they start acting weirdly, this expression might fit them perfectly.

Have Your Cake and Eat It Too

You can either go to a movie or get pizza, but you can't have your cake and eat it too.

Meaning: to spend or use something up but still have it; to have two things when you must choose one

Origin: This saying started sometime in the 1540s. Once you've eaten a piece of cake, you don't have it anymore. So you have to make a decision to eat it or save it. In the same way, money that you've spent is money that you no longer have in your pocket. You have to choose what to do with what you have. The original version of this expression is "you can't eat your cake and have it too."

Have Your Heart in Your Mouth

"My heart was in my mouth when I reached the top of the roller coaster."

Meaning: to be extremely frightened about something

Origin: Homer used this expression thousands of years ago in his famous epic poem the *Iliad*. When you are terrified, your heart starts pounding violently and there's a choking feeling in your throat. Homer referred to that feeling as having "your heart in your mouth." For centuries that's the way many people have described the feeling of extreme terror or dread.

Head and Shoulders Above Someone

"When it comes to aerobics, Lou is head and shoulders above everyone else."

Meaning: far superior; much better than

Origin: When it was first used in the 1800s, this saying referred to height: a very tall person towers over a very short one. But over the years the meaning has been stretched to include any skill one has that is better than someone else's. So a five-foot person may be head and shoulders above a six-foot person in math, tap dancing, and writing stories.

Head Honcho

Do what the head honcho tells you if you want to keep your job.

Meaning: the person in charge; the chief, boss, leader

Origin: The Japanese word *hanchu* means "squad leader" (*han*=squad, *chu*=chief). During the Korean War (1950–53), American soldiers changed the spelling to honcho, and added "head," probably because *head honcho* made a catchy phrase. Today, a head honcho is the principal of a school, the owner of a business, or anyone in charge.

Head in the Clouds

"My report card said that I should pay more attention in class—that my head was usually in the clouds.

Meaning: absent-minded; daydreaming; lost in thought

Origin: In the mid-1600s the idea was first written that if you weren't aware of what was going on, if your mind was in a dreamy state, then your head was in the air. Later "air" was changed to "clouds" because air goes all the way down to the ground but clouds are usually high up. When your "head is in the clouds," it means your mind is definitely somewhere else.

Head over Heels in Love

"He fell head over heels in love with his piano teacher."

Meaning: completely and helplessly in love

Origin: This expression goes back to the ancient Romans and means that being in love with someone makes one's emotions topsy-turvy, upside-down. For nearly 500 years, it was "heels over head." Then, the saying grew to suggest that being in love is like somersaulting.

Heart's in the Right Place

"Kevin messes up sometimes, but his heart's in the right place."

Meaning: to be well-meaning and kindhearted; to have good intentions even though mistakes occur

Origin: Everyone's heart is right in the middle of the chest. Since the heart is often considered the center of one's emotions and feelings, this expression means that even if what you try to do comes out wrong, your intentions are right.

Heavens to Betsy

A 100-year-old woman just flew a plane by herself from New York to California. Heavens to Betsy!

Meaning: an expression of astonishment, amazement, and disbelief

Origin: This expression is a real mystery. We know what it means, and we think it originated in the United States in the late 1890s. But nobody today is 100 percent certain where it came from. Why "heavens"? Who was "Betsy"? Even the word expert who titled his book of curious sayings *Heavens to Betsy!* couldn't name the source.

High Horse

"I wish that new girl in drama class would get down off her high horse."

Meaning: acting superior and arrogant as if you were better than other people

Origin: This saying goes back at least to the early 1700s. In the 14th century, during ceremonial marches and royal exhibitions, well-known people of high rank and superior position in society often rode on large horses that were taller than the average horse. From that custom grew the idea that a person who acts haughty, proud, or snobby is on a "high horse."

Highway Robbery

"Two hundred dollars for one night in a hotel? That's highway robbery!"

Meaning: an extremely high price or charge for something

Origin: During the time of William Shakespeare and the early 16th century, it was common for travelers on the open road to be held up and robbed by armed highwaymen. With time, the phrase "highway robbery" came to be associated with charges for goods and services that were so expensive that the buyer felt that he or she was being robbed by the seller.

Hit Below the Belt

"Saying I shouldn't be president of the Health Club because I'm a little overweight is really hitting below the belt."

Meaning: to use unfair tactics or be unsportsmanlike

Origin: In 1865 in England, the Marquis of Queensberry laid down strict rules for boxing. One of the strictest was that you were not permitted to hit anyone below the belt line. Today that rule still holds in boxing, but the saying also means to act unfairly in any kind of contest, relationship, or activity.

Hit the Books

I've got a major test tomorrow, so I better hit the books.

Meaning: study school assignments carefully; prepare for classes by reading and doing homework

Origin: This idiom says that when you really study hard, you "hit" the books. Why hit? Hit has many meanings. Among them are to come into contact with something forcefully ("The bomb hit its target") and to achieve something you desire ("He hit upon the right formula").

Hit the Hay

It's been a long day, and now it's time to hit the hay.

Meaning: to go to bed

Origin: This slang expression was first used by homeless people who traveled from place to place on foot in the United States in the 1930s. In those days wanderers asked for odd jobs, often begged for money, and were always looking for a place to spend the night. Sometimes they slept on a pile of hay in a field or barn. When their heads "hit the hay," they were probably so tired that they fell asleep quickly. Today, wherever you sleep or whatever you sleep on, when you go to bed, you're hitting the hay.

Hit the Jackpot

"Today I hit the jackpot: I got the highest grade on the spelling test."

Meaning: to be very lucky; to achieve amazing success

Origin: In 19th-century America, when this phrase was first used, if you "hit the jackpot" in a card game, you won all the money. Today the saying refers to any kind of lucky success in any area of life.

Hit the Nail Right on the Head

"When she said that Kirk had the face of a movie star and the brain of a flea, she hit the nail right on the head."

Meaning: to be exactly correct about a description or come to the right conclusion

Origin: The ancient Romans had a similar saying in Latin, and the expression first appeared in English in a book printed in 1508. When hammering, if you hit the nail right on the head, and the nail goes straight in, you've done the job. So if you speak the most accurate words or come to the most sensible conclusion, you "hit the nail on the head."

Hit the Road

"Campers, it's time to hit the road on our fifteen-mile hike."

Meaning: to begin a journey, to leave

Origin: One definition of hit is "to make contact with." Unless you can fly, something must be in contact with the road when moving on it—the rubber on the tires, the soles of shoes, the hooves of the horse. So, when you start out on a journey overland, you're "hitting the road."

Hit the Roof

"When Chad's grandmother saw that he had used her fur coat in his science experiment, she hit the roof."

Meaning: to lose your temper suddenly; to become violently angry

Origin: This frequently used expression comes from early 20th-century America. Imagine a person becoming so angry that she explodes and her body actually hits the roof. It creates a dramatic picture of anger. Other similarly explosive expressions are "hit the ceiling," "blow your top," and "blow your stack."

Hit the Spot

After that long hike through the desert, a cold soda hit the spot.

Meaning: to fully satisfy and refresh, especially with food or drink

Origin: This bit of American slang from the mid-1900s reminds one of "hit the nail right on the head" (see page 92). Imagine that there's a spot inside of you that is the main source of hunger and thirst. Whatever you eat or drink that satisfies your appetite and dry throat "hits the spot." It refreshes your spirits and picks up your strength.

Hitch Your Wagon to a Star

"Even though Paul was small, he hitched his wagon to a star and made it to the top of the league."

Meaning: to aim high; to try to reach the highest level; to follow a great ambition

Origin: Some word experts think that the famous American writer Ralph Waldo Emerson first used this expression in an essay he wrote in 1870. "Hitch" means attach. "Wagon" stands for any vehicle that takes you places. "Star" symbolizes the highest place to which a person can aspire. So if you're ambitious and set high goals for yourself, you're "hitching your wagon to a star."

Hold the Fort

Our teacher was late, so the teacher next door held the fort in our room until he showed up.

Meaning: to temporarily be responsible for watching over a place; to fight off trouble or keep watch

Origin: This expression comes from the military. It was widely used in books and early movies about the old West. Often when a fort was being attacked by enemies on the frontier or during the Civil War, the soldiers defending it were told, "Hold the fort. Don't give up. Help is on its way." Today you can "hold the fort" by watching the children in someone's house until a parent returns or by taking care of a store while the owner's away.

Hold Your Horses

"Hold your horses. Why are you walking so fast?"

Meaning: slow down; wait a minute; be patient

Origin: This 19th-century Americanism originated as an instruction to a carriage driver who was letting his team of horses go too fast. By pulling back on the reins, the driver could slow the horses to a stop. This was called "holding the horses." The saying might also have come from harness racing. Rookie drivers often started their horses too soon, and the starter had to yell, "Hold your horses!" Today the phrase refers to slowing down and being patient in whatever you're doing.

Horse of a Different Color

"I gave her a bus token, but when she wanted me to pay for the movies, too, that was a horse of a different color."

Meaning: a different matter altogether; something from a different nature from that being noticed

Origin: William Shakespeare used a similar phrase in his play *Twelfth Night*, written in 1601. Some people think this expression may have come from betting on a racehorse of one color and then a horse of another color won. Whatever the origin of this saying, "horse" stands for an idea and "different color" (sometimes "another color") means a new thought. In the famous movie *The Wizard of Oz* (1939), Dorothy actually rode around in the Emerald City in a buggy pulled by a horse that kept changing colors. She was told that it was the "horse of a different color."

Hot under the Collar

Better say good night. My father is starting to get hot under the collar.

Meaning: very angry; upset

Origin: Though this expression became popular in the 1800s, it has been observed for centuries that when people become angry, their faces and necks tend to turn red. And under their collars, their necks are getting hot. You'd better watch out! They might blow their stacks.

If the Shoe Fits, Wear It

"Some students never clean up after art class. I'm not mentioning names, but if the shoe fits, wear it."

Meaning: If a remark applies to you, you should admit that it is true.

Origin: This proverb comes from an older expression popular in the 1700s, "If the cap fits, put it on." The "cap" referred to was a dunce cap. As the years went by, the "cap" in the saying changed to "slipper," perhaps because of the popularity of the story of Cinderella. A playwright in the early 1900s wrote, "If the slipper fits, wear it." Later "slipper" changed to "shoe." The idea is clear: Accept a comment that refers to you as you would wear a shoe that fits your foot.

Ignorance Is Bliss

"The bad news can wait until tomorrow. Sometimes, ignorance is bliss."

Meaning: it is better not to know bad news sometimes, especially if you're happy

Origin: Many writers over the centuries have expressed this idea. The Greek playwright Sophocles wrote it around 400 B.C. Nineteen hundred years later Erasmus, a Dutch scholar, quoted it. Then Thomas Gray, the British poet of the 1700s, used it in one of his poems. He wrote: "Where ignorance is bliss, 'tis folly to be wise." It has been a popular saying ever since.

In a Nutshell

In a nutshell, tell me what the show was about.

Meaning: in very few words; briefly; clearly and to the point

Origin: A nutshell, even a big nutshell, is a small space. Not many words can fit into a nutshell, even if you write them in your smallest handwriting or type them.

In Hot Water

"Raul got in hot water with the coach when he missed three practices in a row."

Meaning: in serious trouble or in an embarrassing situation with someone of authority

Origin: This popular expression was being used as early as the 1500s. It may refer to the fact that if you're cooking and you accidentally spill scalding water on yourself, you'll be in trouble. Or it could refer to the ancient custom of pouring a pot of boiling water on intruders as a way of chasing them off. In any case, hot water is definitely something you want to stay out of—unless it's a bubble bath!

In the Bag

The quarterback thinks that the state championship is in the bag.

Meaning: certain of success; fixed

Origin: In the 1600s hunters used to stuff the small birds and animals they had shot into their game bags. A successful hunter had his catch "in the bag." Also, in cockfighting, the game birds were transported to the battle scene in bags. An owner, confident of his bird, would say that victory was "in the bag." By the first half of the 20th century this expression had come to mean a "sure win."

In the Doghouse

"My mother forgot it was my father's birthday, so she's in the doghouse."

Meaning: in disgrace or dislike; facing punishment

Origin: This might have come from the old custom of banishing a bad dog outside to its doghouse. Or it could have originated with the story of Peter Pan, in which Mr. Darling treats the beloved pet dog badly and his children fly off with Peter Pan. Mr. Darling feels so guilty that he lives in the doghouse until his children return home.

In the Driver's Seat

Now that Mr. Bender is retired from the company, his son is in the driver's seat.

Meaning: in control; in the position of authority

Origin: The person sitting in the driver's seat of a car is in charge of the driving. This American idiom from the 20th century, when cars became popular, can be extended from automobiles to any area of life. Whoever is in the driver's seat—the principal, the owner of the company, the President of the United States, and so on—is the person who "calls the shots" (see page 26). A related expression is "backseat driver" (see page 6).

In the Limelight

"Mario loves to be in the limelight. Wait until he sees his picture on the front page."

Meaning: at the center of attention

Origin: All theaters today have powerful electric spotlights that throw bright beams of light on featured performers. In many theaters, beginning in the 1840s, the beam was created by heating lime, a form of calcium oxide, until it produced brilliant white light. A strong lens directed it onto the dancer, juggler, actor, or singer on stage. Anyone "in the limelight" was the center of the audience's attention. Today, we say that a person who gets a lot of attention, especially from the media, is "in the limelight."

In the Pink

"I was pleased to see that old Zack's in the pink."

Meaning: in excellent health physically and emotionally

Origin: Centuries ago "pink" was the name for a popular garden flower. The meaning of the word changed over the years to mean a thing or person at its best. Then William Shakespeare used "pink" in one of his plays (around 1600) to mean perfection. And by the early 1900s, "pink" referred to health, probably because a rosy or pink complexion is a sign of good health.

In the Same Boat

Look, we're all in the same boat, and we've got to work together.

Meaning: in the same bad situation; sharing the same problem or difficulty

Origin: Ever since this saying was first used by ancient Greeks, people have known that all passengers in the same boat, from a sailboat to an ocean liner, share the same possible risks. Over the centuries, the meaning of the expression came to include all people in similar, unpleasant circumstances on land, on sea, or in the air.

It Takes Two to Tango

"It takes two to tango. Who was your accomplice?"

Meaning: two people are required to accomplish this deed

Origin: In the United States in the 1920s, the Latin American dance called the tango became popular, and so did this expression. Just as it takes two dancers to do the tango, there are certain activities that need the cooperation of two people in order to work. For many books, one person writes the words and another draws the pictures. There are a lot of other activities in which it "takes two to tango."

Jack-of-all-Trades

"Our handyman is a jack-of-all-trades. He can fix anything."

Meaning: a person who can do many different kinds of work well

Origin: A worker who is capable of doing many craft-type tasks well (painting, electrical work, plumbing, and so on) has been called a "jack-of-all-trades" since the 1600s. "Jack" is an informal word for "trade laborer." A longer version of this expression is "A jack of all trades and master of none," which means someone who knows how to do a lot of things pretty well but who is not an expert at any of them. The longer version started being used in the latter half of the 19th century.

Jet Set

My Aunt Ida, on her farm in Iowa, loves to read about the jet set.

Meaning: the wealthy, fashionable, and famous people who travel frequently

Origin: "Jet" refers to jet planes. "Set" is a group of people. After the introduction of travel by swift jet planes in the late 1950s, the term "jet set" caught on to describe rich and fashionable people who rarely stayed in one place for any length of time. They were always flying off to a party in Hollywood, or to a luxurious home in Spain. Today, to be a member of the jet set, you just have to be a member of high society. The fact that "jet" and "set" rhyme helped make this a widely used phrase.

Jump down Your Throat

"All I said was, 'Could you not give us homework tonight, Mr. Brill,' and he jumped down my throat."

Meaning: to talk or scream at someone in a sudden, angry way

Origin: This saying has been popular since the early 1800s. If someone jumps at you, they suddenly and quickly spring off the ground. Your larynx and vocal chords, which produce speech, are located in your throat. So if you say something that angers someone, then he or she would be "jumping down your throat" by suddenly scolding you.

Jump Off the Deep End

"Ed and Esther just met, but they're getting married. They're jumping off the deep end."

Meaning: to act emotionally without carefully thinking about the end result; to become deeply involved before you're ready to

Origin: People should not jump into the deep end of a swimming pool if they are not 100 percent sure that they can swim. It's better to start in the shallow end and swim to the deeper side. (See "get your feet wet," page 76.) But if people follow their emotions without much thought, they could be in deep water and in over their heads. Since the early 1900s "jump off the deep end" has also meant going into a rage or having a mental breakdown.

Jump on the Bandwagon

"Last year nobody liked my idea of a school carnival. Now everyone wants to jump on the bandwagon."

Meaning: to become part of the newest activity because many other people are

Origin: Many years ago candidates for political office in the United States often rode through town in horse-drawn wagons on which a band was playing music to attract a crowd. If the candidate was popular, people would jump up onto his bandwagon to show their support. Today we say that people who are getting involved in any activity that looks like it's going to succeed are "jumping on the bandwagon."

Jump the Gun

I couldn't wait to give my mother her Mother's Day gift, so I jumped the gun and gave it to her a week early.

Meaning: to do or say something before you should; to act prematurely or hastily

Origin: In the early 1900s this expression was "to beat the pistol." It referred to someone starting a race before the starter's pistol was fired. Later the saying changed to "jump the gun," perhaps because of the repetition of the "u" sound in the middle of "jump" and "gun."

Keep a Stiff Upper Lip

"Even when the boss yelled at Nyasha for dropping the soup in the lady's lap, she kept a stiff upper lip."

Meaning: to be brave and not show emotion in a time of trouble

Origin: This American expression was first used in the early 1800s. When a person is frightened or angry or ready to burst into tears, his or her lips often tremble. So if you're told to "keep a stiff upper lip," someone wants you to hide your feelings. You may wonder why the idiom refers only to the upper lip and not to both lips. It might have to do with the fact that in the 1800s, when many men grew mustaches, a trembling upper lip was more noticeable. A similar expression is "keep your chin up."

Keep a Straight Face

When you see Ms. Navarro's new haircut, try to keep a straight face.

Meaning: to keep from laughing

Origin: This is a recent idiom. When you laugh, your face wrinkles, your mouth opens wide, your eyebrows rise, and your facial muscles twist and turn. Your face is anything but "straight."

Keep Body and Soul Together

"He got a job that paid so little, he was barely able to keep body and soul together."

Meaning: to keep alive; to have just enough to survive

Origin: In the early 18th century, people were beginning to use this expression. Those who lose their money and possessions often also lose their self-respect. But if they earn just enough money to clothe, house, and feed themselves, though they may not have a fancy house or expensive things, at least they will always have their body and soul. A related idiom is "keep the wolf from the door" (see page 103).

Keep Something under Your Hat

I'll tell you who won the election, but you've got to keep the results under your hat.

Meaning: to keep something secret

Origin: This expression comes from the late 1800s, when many more men and women wore hats than they do today. Your head is under your hat. So if someone tells you to keep a bit of news under your hat, he or she is telling you to keep it in your head and not reveal it to anyone else.

Keep the Wolf from the Door

"He got two extra jobs just to keep the wolf from the door."

Meaning: to keep from suffering poverty or starvation

Origin: Wolves have always been extremely hungry, hunting animals. People are rightfully afraid of the big, bad wolf. Poverty and starvation are as scary as a wolf. Since the 16th century, people have been saying that if you have just enough to get by, you're "keeping the wolf from the door." A related idiom is "keep body and soul together."

Keep Up with the Joneses

"The man next door got a new car, so my cousin got one too. He has to keep up with the Joneses."

Meaning: to try to keep up with what your neighbors have socially and financially; to work hard to have possessions as good as your neighbors

Origin: In 1913 a popular comic strip called "Keeping Up with the Joneses" appeared in many American newspapers, starting with the New York *Globe*. The cartoon was about the experiences of a newly married young man, and the cartoonist based it on his own life. He chose the name Jones because it was a popular name in America. The name of the comic strip became a popular expression that meant to try hard to follow the latest fashion and live in the style of those around you.

Keep Your Ear to the Ground

"Years ago my uncle kept his ear to the ground and invested in cable TV, and today he's a millionaire."

Meaning: to pay attention and be well-informed

Origin: In the late 1800s, when this expression first came into use, European Americans and Native Americans often fought. To tell if the enemy was riding toward them on horseback, people would actually put an ear right to the ground. They could often hear the sound of the hooves of approaching horses. Today this expression means to watch and listen closely to signs that might show the way things will go in the future.

Keep Your Fingers Crossed

"We need a home run to win. Keep your fingers crossed."

Meaning: to wish for good luck and success for someone or something

Origin: This old American expression may come from the superstition that the cross works to keep away evil and bad luck. It may also come from children's games in which the players crossed their fingers to keep safe. Today, some people believe that if they cross their fingers when they tell a lie, the lie doesn't "count."

Keep Your Head above Water

Business is bad this season, and Dad is barely keeping his head above water.

Meaning: to earn enough to stay out of debt and avoid financial ruin; to do just enough to keep up with all of one's responsibilities

Origin: In several idioms, water represents possible trouble. Think of "jump off the deep end" (see page 101), "between the devil and the deep blue sea" (see page 12), and "pour oil on troubled waters" (see page 149). The idiom "keep your head above water" hints at the risk of drowning. "Water," in this case, represents going bankrupt or being ruined financially.

Keep Your Nose to the Grindstone

"My grandfather told me that if I wanted to succeed I had better keep my nose to the grindstone."

Meaning: to force oneself to work hard all the time; to always keep busy

Origin: Erasmus, a Dutch scholar, used a similar saying in the 1500s. A grindstone is a revolving stone disk used for polishing or sharpening tools or grinding grain. To see what you're doing while you work a grindstone you have to bend over it with your face close to the stone. The image of a person with his or her "nose to the grindstone" has come to mean working nonstop over a long period of time, often at a long and tiring job. The nose is used in many idioms: "by a nose," "keep your nose clean," "no skin off one's nose" (see page 126), "nose around in something," "nose out of joint," "on the nose," "pay through the nose (see page 144)."

Keep Your Shirt on

The referee saw the two players shouting at each other and told them to keep their shirts on.

Meaning: to remain cool; to not become angry; to be patient

Origin: In the mid-1800s, when this saying first came into use, a man who was going to get into a fistfight with someone often took his shirt off. It wasn't easy to fight in a stiff, starched shirt, and if you took it off, it wouldn't get wrinkled, dirty, or bloody.

Kick the Bucket

"During the summer my Mom's 1970 Thunderbird kicked the bucket."

Meaning: to die

Origin: This expression was used in England as early as the 16th century. It came from the practice of hanging a criminal by having him stand on a bucket, putting a noose around his neck, and then kicking the bucket out from under him. Prisoners who committed suicide by hanging themselves in their cells sometimes kicked a bucket out from under their own legs. Today this slang expression can be applied to any manner of death.

Kick Up Your Heels

On graduation night, Alex is going to kick up his heels until dawn.

Meaning: to celebrate and have a wonderful time

Origin: This way of describing a happy person having great fun dates from the late 19th or early 20th century. The person who made it up was probably thinking of a lively horse prancing on its hind legs, or of a dancer lifting his or her legs as if jumping for joy.

Kill the Goose that Lays the Golden Eggs

"Don't be obnoxious to Aunt Ruthie when she gives you money. You'll kill the goose that lays the golden egg."

Meaning: to spoil or destroy something good out of stupidity, greed, or impatience

Origin: There's a fable by Aesop about a farmer who owns a goose that lays one golden egg at a time. The greedy farmer becomes impatient and kills the goose so he can get all the eggs that are in the goose at once. Of course, a dead goose can't lay any more eggs, as the foolish farmer soon finds out. In 15th-century England, the plot of this well-known story helped create the famous phrase, "kill the goose that laid the golden eggs."

Kill Two Birds with One Stone

"At the library, Niko can kill two birds with one stone. He does his schoolwork and sees his friends."

Meaning: to do two things by one action; to get two results with just one effort

Origin: There was a similar expression in Latin about 2,000 years ago, and "kill two birds with one stone" became popular in English many centuries later. It comes from hunting birds by throwing stones at them or shooting stones at them with a slingshot. If you actually killed two birds with just one stone, a practically impossible feat, you'd be carrying out two tasks with just a single effort.

Knee-High to a Grasshopper

"Mr. Fernandez always reminds me that he knew me when I was just knee-high to a grasshopper."

Meaning: very young and, therefore, very short

Origin: This American expression was first recorded in 1814 as "knee-high to a toad." Some people said knee-high to a toad, mosquito, bumblebee, or duck. Some even said "splinter," which definitely doesn't have knees but is small. "Grasshopper" caught on about 1850 because they definitely have knees, and the saying stuck. To come up to the knee of a grasshopper, one would be less than an inch tall!

Knock on Wood

So far, the new teacher doesn't give too much homework. Knock on wood.

Meaning: an expression said when knocking on wood in order to keep from having bad luck

Origin: In England people say "touch wood" when they want to head off bad luck. Although "knock on wood" is a popular expression, nobody today is certain of where it came from. Experts think it may have originated from the time of the ancient Druids, an order of Celtic priests in Ireland and Britain. Whatever the origin, you'll often see people knocking on wood to keep away bad luck or help prevent a change of fortune from good to bad.

Labor of Love

"He didn't get paid for painting the nursing home. It was a labor of love."

Meaning: work done not for money but for love or a sense of accomplishment

Origin: In the New Testament of the Bible there is a phrase about work done for pleasure without profit, "your work of faith and labor of love." The English expression "labor of love" became popular around the 17th century, when many people worked at something because they loved doing it and not for money. Also, "labor" and "love" both begin with the letter "l," and that alliteration helped make the expression easy to remember.

Laugh Out of the other Side of Your Mouth

"Once the news gets out that Sid bought votes to win the election, he'll be laughing out of the other side of his mouth."

Meaning: to be made to feel sorrow, annoyance, or disappointment after you felt happy; to cry at a change in luck after experiencing some happiness

Origin: This saying was being used in England in the 17th century. This expression might not seem to make much sense. When a person laughs, he or she does it from both sides of the mouth. You wouldn't laugh at all if you didn't feel happy. The key words in the phrase are "other side." The other side of happiness is sadness, and the idiom suggests that by laughing on the other or wrong side of your mouth, or face, your fortune has gone bad and your moment of happiness is over.

Lay an Egg

Who told Sam she could sing? She really laid an egg at the talent show.

Meaning: to give an embarrassing performance

Origin: This idiom comes from Britain, where cricket has been a popular game for centuries. If a team failed to score a single point, people said it had laid a duck's egg, an object that has the same shape as the 0 on the scoreboard. In the United States, toward the end of the 1800s, the saying "laid an egg" was applied to performers in vaudeville shows who bombed in front of the audience. In baseball slang, the expression for "zero" is "goose egg," and to get no score is to "lay a goose egg." Today you can "lay an egg" if you do anything that fails totally because nobody likes it.

Lay Your Cards on the Table

"The mayor laid the cards on the table about his secret campaign funds."

Meaning: to reveal all the facts openly and honestly; to reveal one's purpose and plans

Origin: This is another idiom that comes from playing cards. There are many games in which players have to put their cards on the table face up to show what cards they have been holding. When that happens, there are no secrets, the truth is out.

Lead You by the Nose

"My grandfather thinks he's boss, but everyone knows that Grandma really leads him by the nose."

Meaning: to dominate or control someone

Origin: Animals, like cattle in the field or trained bears in a circus, are often led about by a rope attached to a ring in their noses. Phrases about being led by your nose first appeared in the Bible (Isaiah 37:29) and later in English about A.D. 170. By the 1500s the saying was carried over to people who were controlled by other people.

Leave No Stone Unturned

She vowed that she would leave no stone unturned in finding out who let the air out of her tires.

Meaning: to make all possible efforts to carry out a task or search for someone or something

Origin: Euripides, a great playwright of ancient Greece, once told the legend of a Persian general who left a treasure in his tent and then lost a major battle. Someone went looking for the treasure but couldn't find it, so he went to the Oracle of Delphi for advice. The oracle said, *Movere omnem lapidum* which meant "Move every stone" in Latin.

L

Leave Someone Holding the Bag

When the teacher demanded to know who wrote the joke on the blackboard, Diego was left holding the bag.

Meaning: to force someone to take the blame when it should be shared

Origin: This expression was known by many Americans in the 1780s. It might have come from a mean trick boys played on a new boy in town. They'd take him to the woods at night, give him a lantern and a bag, and tell him to wait for a bird that, attracted by the light, would fly into the bag. The rest of the boys would return home, knowing no bird would appear.

Left Out in the Cold

"Christina told everyone else about the party, but she left me out in the cold."

Meaning: to not tell someone something; to exclude someone from a place or activity

Origin: If someone locked the door and left you outside on a cold night, you would feel excluded and ignored. When this expression first became popular, it meant exactly that: literally being left outside in cold weather.

Lend an Ear

"I know you're very busy, but could you just lend me your ear for a minute?"

Meaning: to listen and pay attention to

Origin: This saying, of course, doesn't really mean to lend someone your ears as you would lend him or her a pencil. In William Shakespeare's time, around 1600, it was a common way of asking that you listen to the person speaking. Shakespeare used this expression in the play *Julius Caesar* when he had his character Mark Antony shout to a noisy crowd of Romans at the funeral of the assassinated Julius Caesar, "Friends, Romans, countrymen, lend me your ears." The crowd quickly quieted and listened to what Mark Antony had to say. The expression caught on.

Let Sleeping Dogs Lie

"Don't remind the director that you missed two rehearsals. Better to let sleeping dogs lie."

Meaning: to not make trouble if you don't have to; to not make someone angry by stirring up trouble

Origin: This well-known proverb was used by many people in the 1200s. English writer Geoffrey Chaucer used it in one of his books in 1374, saying it was not good to wake a sleeping dog. Imagine that you come upon a sleeping dog. Since you don't know what will happen if you wake it up (it may pounce on you and bite you!), it would be much smarter to just let the hound dream on. In the same way, if right now everything is calm, it's better not to stir up anything that could cause trouble or danger. Leave well enough alone!

Let the Cat Out of the Bag

"Carol's little brother let the cat out of the bag about her surprise party."

Meaning: to give away a secret

Origin: Centuries ago in England you might have bought a costly pig at a farmer's market. But if the merchant was dishonest and put a worthless cat into the bag instead of a piglet, you might not find out until you got home and let the cat out of the bag. Related expressions are "buy a pig in a poke" (see page 24) and "spill the beans" (see page 179) .

Let the Chips Fall where They May

I will speak out against the new dress code and let the chips fall where they may.

Meaning: to do the right thing, as you see it, whatever the consequences might be

Origin: This idiom was first used in the 1880s and referred to woodcutters who needed to concentrate on doing a good job instead of on where the small chips of wood fell from their axes.

Let Your Hair Down

"At my sleep-over party, Nina really let her hair down."

Meaning: to behave freely and naturally; to relax and show your true self

Origin: This idiom started in the 1800s when many women wore their long hair pinned up in public and only let it down in private, especially just before they went to bed.

Light at the End of the Tunnel

After many years of experiments on the phonograph, Edison saw the light at the end of the tunnel with the wax cylinder.

Meaning: a long-searched-for answer, goal, or success

Origin: Imagine driving through a long, dark tunnel. You wonder when you'll ever get out. Then, far ahead, you see a tiny spot of light that marks the end of the tunnel. You know that if you keep going forward, the light will grow bigger and you will come out into the sunlight again. Now imagine that the tunnel represents a long period of hard work. The light represents the end of that work. It's still up ahead, but it gives you hope to continue your quest.

Like a Bump on a Log

"Don't just sit there like a bump on a log. Help me move this piano."

Meaning: inactive and not responding

Origin: Mark Twain, the author of *Tom Sawyer* and *Huckleberry Finn*, among other great books, used this simile (a comparison often using "like" or "as") in 1863. A bump on a log is an immovable lump of wood. In this idiom it represents a fixed, motionless person.

Like It or Lump It

"If you miss one word, you're out of the spelling bee. Like it or lump it."

Meaning: whether you like it or not; certain to happen

Origin: This American saying comes from the early 1800s. Where does "lump" come from? Perhaps from a verb in British dialect, "to lump," which means to look gloomy, sulky, and cranky. You can resent what happens, or you can try to like, or at least accept, something because it is certain to happen.

Like Two Peas in a Pod

"Kyle and his brother are like two peas in a pod."

Meaning: identical; alike in looks and behavior

Origin: A pod is a seedcase that holds beans or peas. When it is ripe, the pod splits open to let go of what's inside. Peas lying cozily in a pod seem alike in shape and color.

Little Pitchers Have Big Ears

My big sister and her friends never tell secrets around me. They say that little pitchers have big ears.

Meaning: little children, listening to the conversations of older people, often hear and understand a lot more than people give them credit for

Origin: The creator of this ancient saying imagined that the handles on the sides of a two-handled pitcher looked like human ears. The little pitchers in this idiom stand for small children, and having big ears means they are able to hear and understand things adults think they're too young to know.

Live High off the Hog

"Since Florence got a new job, she's been living high off the hog."

Meaning: to live in a rich style and own lots of expensive things

Origin: This African-American expression suggests that eating pork chops and ribs, which come from the upper parts of a hog, are better than eating pig feet, chitlins (intestines), and other things that come from the lower parts.

Lock, Stock, and Barrel

"He sold everything—lock, stock, and barrel—and moved to California."

Meaning: the whole of something; all the parts of a thing; everything

Origin: This saying originally referred to just the three main parts of a gun: the lock (the firing mechanism), the stock (the handle), and the barrel (the tube the bullet is fired through). By the early 19th century the expression came to mean all of anything or the whole works. The origin might also be in the old general store, which had a lock on the door to the stock, or goods, and a barrel on which business took place.

Lock the Barn Door after the Horse Is Out

If you failed the quiz, why study? That's locking the barn door after the horse is out!

Meaning: to take careful precautions to do the right thing after it is too late

Origin: This popular proverb can be found in many languages. It was first used in French in the 1100s and later appeared in English. If you put a prize horse into the barn for the night and then forgot to lock the door, it is possible that the next day you'll find the horse is gone or stolen. It would be pretty foolish to lock the barn door then, because the horse is already gone.

Long in the Tooth

"Grandma's boyfriend looks a little long in the tooth, even for her."

Meaning: old; aged

Origin: This 19th-century idiom comes from the barnyard. As a horse gets older, its gums move back and the teeth appear longer. So a horse that is "long in the tooth" is getting old. This expression was passed on to people.

Look down Your Nose at Someone

The eleventh-graders looked down their noses at us.

Meaning: to think of and treat people as if they were lower in quality or ability

Origin: From about 1700 "to look down" at someone meant to believe that you were better in quality or rank than another. "Nose" was added about 200 years later. The saying creates a clear image: A person who thinks he or she is above others actually looks down his or her nose at someone in a proud and self-important way.

Lose Your Shirt

"Spiro lost his shirt betting against me in the frog-jumping contest."

Meaning: to lose everything, especially money

Origin: This 20th-century phrase refers to a huge loss of money or property because of a bad bet or poorly managed money. If you end up losing your shirt, it means you've lost practically everything. But the idiom started out meaning "to be very angry" and ready to fight.

Low Man on the Totem Pole

"I may be low man on the totem pole, but someday I plan to be Chief Executive Officer."

Meaning: the lowest-ranking, least important person in a group or organization

Origin: Some Native American groups carve symbols, one on top of the other, into tall poles of wood. The symbols, called totems, are often human faces or figures, and the pole is called a totem pole. Although "lowest" often means "least" in phrases like "lowest pay" and "lowest score," the lowest face on a totem pole is not the least important. The person who created this idiom must have thought so by mistake. But few people realize the error when they use this popular saying.

Lower the Boom

When the counselor saw that the campers had put frogs in his bed, he lowered the boom on them.

Meaning: to scold or punish strictly; to make someone follow the rules

Origin: A boom is a long pole used on ships that stretches upward to lift cargo high in the air. Booms are also used backstage in theaters to move scenery. If someone actually lowered a boom on your head, you might be knocked out!

Mad as a Hatter

Sean is as mad as a hatter, but he's my most interesting friend.

Meaning: completely crazy, strange, eccentric

Origin: Lewis Carroll created the character of the Mad Hatter in his classic book *Alice in Wonderland*. The expression "mad as a hatter" comes from the early 1800s. One possible origin is a snake called an adder. People in England thought that if you were bitten by an adder, its poison would make you insane. Some people pronounced "adder" as "atter," so if you acted crazy, you were as "mad as an atter," which later became "hatter." Another explanation of the expression's origin is that people who worked in felt-hat factories in the 1800s inhaled fumes of mercuric nitrate, and, as a result, developed twitches, jumbled their speech, and grew confused. The condition was sometimes mistaken for madness and may have given birth to the saying "mad as a hatter."

Mad as a Wet Hen

"When Tess realized that her brother had eaten all the cookies, she was as mad as a wet hen."

Meaning: very upset; extremely angry; ready to fight

Origin: It doesn't really bother hens much when they get wet. This early 19th century expression probably resulted from a mistake or someone's imagination. It is not a barnyard reality.

Make a Federal Case out of Something

"I was looking at your test paper to see the date. Don't make a federal case out of it."

Meaning: to exaggerate the seriousness of something small; to make a big deal out of something

Origin: The federal courts and Supreme Court of the United States handle the most important issues of the law. So, if you overreact to something said or done, you're "making a federal case out of it," or making it more important than it needs to be.

Make a Mountain out of a Molehill

"Your 'broken arm' was only a sprained wrist. Don't make a mountain out of a molehill."

Meaning: to turn a small, unimportant issue into a big, important one; to exaggerate the importance of something

Origin: A mountain is huge; a molehill is small. The ancient Greeks had a saying, "make an elephant out of a fly," which became a proverb in French and German. By the mid-1500s people in England were saying "make a mountain out of a molehill," probably because "make," "mountain," and "molehill" all begin with "m," and alliteration helps make an expression fun to say and easier to remember.

Make a Silk Purse out of a Sow's Ear

Owen thinks that by polishing his old car, he can make a silk purse out of a sow's ear.

Meaning: to create something valuable or beautiful out of something practically worthless or ugly

Origin: There are similar expressions in many languages; these sayings also use "good thing-bad thing" combinations (for instance, "good coat out of poor cloth," and "hunting horn out of a pig's tail"). An English version close to this idiom has been around since 1700. A silk purse is an elegant, expensive item made of fine, shiny fibers. A sow is an adult female pig. So if anyone can take a sow's ear and turn it into a silk purse, he or she might be able to take a bad situation and make something good out of it.

Make Ends Meet

"On her salary, Jackie can hardly make ends meet."

Meaning: to earn just enough to live within one's income

Origin: What does "ends" mean in this expression? Some word experts think that in the 1600s it could have meant the sum total, the end of a column of figures that were added up. Others think that in the mid-1700s it meant the beginning and end of the financial year.

Make Hay while the Sun Shines

"If you want a part in the show, you'd better put on your tap shoes and make hay while the sun shines."

Meaning: to make the best of a limited opportunity

Origin: This proverb dates from the early to mid-1500s. Hay is made from grass that has been cut and dried. Rain will spoil cut grass, so farmers have to time it right and make hay on days when the sun is shining. This expression includes anything that should be done when the time is right, taking full advantage of an opportunity before it passes.

Make Heads or Tails out of Something

"Dad couldn't make heads or tails out of the instructions for taping shows with his new VCR."

Meaning: to understand how something works; to figure something out

Origin: Cicero, a Roman statesman and public speaker of the first century B.C., used a similar expression, "neither head nor feet." The current English saying comes from the 1600s. The head is the front or top of something. The tail is the end or bottom. So if you can make heads or tails out of something, you can understand it from beginning to end, from top to bottom. This expression is usually used in the negative ("They can't make...") because there are a lot of things in this world that are difficult to understand.

Make No Bones about Something

The substitute teacher made no bones about not liking hats worn in class.

Meaning: to speak directly, plainly, honestly, and without hesitation or doubt

Origin: The origin of this old idiom, first used in print in 1548, is not clear. Some word experts have suggested that it came from the fact that if there are no bones in your soup, you can just swallow it without worrying about choking. That's like speaking plainly without worrying.

Make Waves

"I don't mean to make waves, but I don't agree with my curfew."

Meaning: to cause trouble; to upset matters; to create a disturbance

Origin: This 20th-century American saying refers to keeping waters still. If you want to sail peacefully on in your sailboat or float calmly on a raft, you don't want anybody making waves. That might rock the boat or even flip your raft over. A related idiom is "rock the boat" (see page 162).

Make Your Mouth Water

"Seeing those posters of Hawaii made my mouth water for a vacation on a beach."

Meaning: to look so attractive and desirable that it makes you want to have it very much; to want to eat or drink something that looks or smells delicious

Origin: This expression was used as early as the mid-1500s, but since time began, people have known that the sight, smell, or even thought of food can make a person's salivary glands start up, causing the mouth to water. Though this saying is often used in connection with food or drink, it can really be used when looking forward to something that you want a lot.

Mess with Someone

Don't even think of messing with the new teacher. She's tough.

Meaning: to annoy, argue with, hassle, or otherwise anger and irritate a person

Origin: This modern African-American expression is similar in meaning to "bug someone" (see page 20). "To mess" is to butt into other people's business or interfere with other people's lives.

Mince Words

"Please don't mince words. Tell me exactly what you think of my painting."

Meaning: to not come right to the point and be honest; to use mild or vague words so as not to offend or hurt someone

Origin: William Shakespeare used this expression in some of his plays in the late 1500s, but it might have been in use before that. Originally "mince" meant to soften or lessen the force of certain words in order to be polite. Today, if you mince words or mince matters, you are not being honest and open.

Mind over Matter

"Nancy ran in the track meet with a twisted ankle—a perfect example of mind over matter."

Meaning: the power of your mind is stronger than the body

Origin: Virgil, a Roman poet who was born in 70 B.C., used this expression in his famous poem, the *Aeneid*. "Mind" means brain, thoughts, and willpower. "Matter" means a physical object, and it can also mean trouble or difficulty. Notice also that "mind" and "matter" both begin with "m," and alliteration helps make a saying more popular.

Mind Your P's And Q's

Please try to mind your P's and Q's when the princess visits the school.

Meaning: to be extremely exact; be careful not to say or do anything wrong; mind your manners

Origin: This term was beginning to be used in the 1600s, and by the late 1700s it was very popular. The letters "p" and "q" can often be confused, so children learning to read and printers selecting type have to be careful with these letters. Another possibility comes from old English pubs where a list of the pints ("p's") and quarts ("q's") a drinker consumed were written on a blackboard to be paid for later. Finally, *pieds* and *queues* are dance steps that a French dancing instructor would teach his students to perform with care. There's no proof as to where this catchy saying originated, though.

Miss the Boat

"If you're late to the interview, you'll miss the boat for the job."

Meaning: to lose an opportunity; to arrive too late and miss out on something

Origin: This expression has been used by many people since about 1900, when there were no airplanes and many people traveled to far-off places by boat. If you arrived at the dock after the boat had sailed because you lost track of time, overslept, or were delayed, then you missed out.

Monkey Business

No more monkey business! Settle down.

Meaning: silliness or fooling around; dishonest or illegal activities; idiotic pranks

Origin: This expression has two meanings. One concerns comical behavior like that of a playful monkey. The other refers to sneaky, unlawful actions. So a student could be sent to the principal's office for monkey business, and a politician can be sent to jail for monkey business. This idiom, from 20th-century America, is like many other expressions that relate human behavior to animal behavior ("sly as a fox," "wise as an owl," and so on), and probably comes from an older expression, "monkeyshines," which dates from the 1820s.

More than Meets the Eye

"Sherlock Holmes realized immediately that there was more to the murder than met the eye."

Meaning: there are hidden facts that can't be seen or understood right away

Origin: This British cliché from the 1800s says that often things have deeper levels of meaning and importance than you can see at first. The full truth of a situation has to be thoroughly investigated. You might have to use a microscope or research skills to uncover the real facts of something.

More than One Way to Skin a Cat

"Scott tried every solution to the puzzle he could think of because he knew there was more than one way to skin a cat."

Meaning: there are several different ways of reaching the same goal

Origin: This American idiom has been in use since the mid-1800s, when removing animals' pelts was more common than it is today. Each person who skinned a cat or animal had his or her own particular way of doing it. Over the years the saying took on broader meaning, and now it can refer to the many methods of accomplishing goals. The original British expression was "there are more ways of killing a cat than choking it with cream."

Mum's the Word

Don't tell anyone about the surprise for Mr. Glick. Remember, mum's the word.

Meaning: you must keep silent; don't tell anyone the secret

Origin: Since at least 1350 "mum" has meant silent. The word itself sounds like a person trying to talk with her lips shut tight. "Mum's the word" has been a popular expression since about 1700.

N

Name Is Mud

"Everyone knows that it was Joseph who started the fight during the game. Now that we're disqualified, his name is mud."

Meaning: the person is in trouble, possibly doomed and worthless

Origin: In the 1700s "mud" was a slang word for "fool" or "stupid person" in England. Starting in the early 1800s, the saying "His name is mud" was used in the British Parliament to point out any member of Parliament who had disgraced himself.

Necessity Is the Mother of Invention

He created shoes with stilts so he could reach the ceiling. Necessity is the mother of invention.

Meaning: inventiveness or creativity is stimulated by need or difficulty

Origin: A phrase similar to this was used by people in ancient Greece, and today it is a proverb in Italian, French, German, and some other languages. The first use of it in English was in a British play in 1672. It's very popular all over the world, probably because it states a universal truth. If you urgently need something that you don't have, you will discover or invent it by using your imagination and skill. In this expression, "mother" means the creative source that gives birth to the invention.

Need Something like a Hole in the Head

"Conchita needed a battery-operated, revolving-head spaghetti fork like she needed a hole in the head."

Meaning: to have no need for something at all

Origin: This bit of American slang comes from the 1940s. It is similar to older sayings that used the idea of not needing something that is totally unnecessary such as "I need this like I need a disease . . . a cough . . . a toad. . . ." and so on. The words "hole in the head" come from a Yiddish expression, *loch in kop.*

Needle in a Haystack

"Looking for your contact lens in this shaggy rug will be like looking for a needle in a haystack."

Meaning: something hard or impossible to find; anything hopeless (in a search)

Origin: Since the early 1500s there have been similar expressions to describe things difficult to find: "like finding a needle in a meadow of hay" and "like finding a pin's head in a cartload of hay." In the mid-1800s the expression became "needle in a haystack." Sayings like these are popular in other languages, too. Finding anything in a haystack is hard, but finding a needle in one is nearly impossible.

Nickel-and-Dime

He said he worked for a big corporation, but it was really only a nickel-and-dime company.

Meaning: unimportant, small-time, trivial, petty

Origin: In this 20th-century African-American saying, "nickel-and-dime" refers to two of the smallest units of United States money. Anything that's "nickel-and-dime" is the opposite of "big bucks." Note: This expression can also be used as a verb meaning to act in a cheap manner, as in "He never takes her to fancy restaurants. He always nickels and dimes her."

Nitty-Gritty

"When you write your report, stick to the nitty-gritty."

Meaning: the specific heart of the matter; the practical details; the fundamental core of something

Origin: Grit means tiny, rough granules of stone or sand. Imagine you're trying to examine or explain something. Instead of wasting time on unimportant subjects, you concentrate on the grit, the small but basic and necessary points. "Nitty-gritty," a 20th-century African-American phrase, is a rhyming extension of the word "grit." "Grit" was stretched to "gritty" and was rhymed with "nitty" to make a colorful, fun phrase.

No Dice

"I asked my father for a raise in my allowance, but he said, 'No dice!'"

Meaning: refused; no! absolutely not

Origin: This 20th-century American saying must come from gambling games that use dice, but no one is sure about the original meaning. If there are no dice, there's no game, which should explain how this phrase came to mean "no!"

No Skin off Your Nose

He doesn't care if I make the football team or not. It's no skin off his nose.

Meaning: of totally no concern to you whatsoever; it doesn't matter to you one way or the other

Origin: This American idiom dates to the 1920s. Originally, the expression was "no skin off my back." "Nose" is more suitable because if you stick your nose into somebody's business, you can get it hurt.

No Spring Chicken

"Grandma can't run and play ball the way she used to. She's no spring chicken."

Meaning: not young anymore

Origin: This saying has been around since the early 1800s, and it almost always applied to women, although there's no reason it couldn't refer to men, too. A spring chicken is a really young chick, like a baby. The expression began as "now past a chicken," and the saying today is a variation of the original.

Not Your Cup of Tea

"Please show me another hat. This one's not my cup of tea."

Meaning: not what one likes or prefers; not suitable; not to your taste

Origin: In Britain, tea has been an extremely popular drink since the mid-1700s. Even now many English people have a cup of tea every mid-afternoon, and there are many different flavors to choose from. In the late 1800s, people in England started saying that something they liked was their "cup of tea." Later, probably in the 1920s, the expression took on its present meaning.

Nothing New under the Sun

"This expensive pasta is really just macaroni. There's nothing new under the sun."

Meaning: everything is just a little different but pretty much the same as an earlier invention

Origin: This expression was more fitting when it first appeared in the Bible. Then, amazing scientific discoveries weren't being announced almost every day. Today, you learn about new things in the world ("under the sun") all the time. This saying can also be used when you see something that's supposed to be new but is really a variation of something old. Advertisers try to convince us that their products are different from earlier items. But if you look closely, you may discover that in some cases there's "nothing new under the sun."

Nothing to Sneeze At

"He won the silver medal, not the gold. That's nothing to sneeze at."

Meaning: not small or unimportant; something to be taken seriously

Origin: In the early 1800s people were already using this saying. Perhaps it comes from the idea of turning your nose up at something or someone to express scorn or contempt. Since sneezes come from your nose, something that's "not to be sneezed at" should be treated as important and worthy.

Nothing Ventured, Nothing Gained

C'mon, try making that dive. Nothing ventured, nothing gained.

Meaning: If you don't try to do something, you'll never accomplish it

Origin: This old proverb states a commonsense truth: If you don't make an effort—even though you may be risking failure—you will never reach your goal. Nothing risked or dared ("ventured"), nothing attained ("gained").

Nutty as a Fruitcake

I was convinced that Brian's uncle was as nutty as a fruitcake.

Meaning: crazy or extremely strange in behavior or dress

Origin: This widely used saying originated in America in the 1920s. "Nutty" was slang for crazy; a "nut" was an eccentric person who seemed abnormal in the way he or she appeared or dressed. Fruitcakes are made with plenty of nuts, so if a person is as "nutty as a fruitcake," he or she is really strange

Off the Beaten Track (Path)

"That restaurant's really off the beaten track but worth the trip."

Meaning: not well-known or used; an unfamiliar location; unusual; different

Origin: In the 1600s, when this idiom was first used, there were many dirt roads. As people walked or rode over them, the paths were beaten down by feet, horses' hooves, and wagon wheels. They looked well used. But if something was "off the beaten track" (or "path"), then few people traveled that way. We now use this expression to describe anything unusual, not often used, or not seen by many people.

Off the Top of Your Head

"Right off the top of his head he listed all the state capitals in alphabetical order."

Meaning: stating something quickly and without thinking hard about it

Origin: In the middle of the 20th century, Americans started using this expression. Thoughts come from your brain, which is in the top of your head. So if you blurt out facts quickly without having to think about them, then you're talking "off the top of your head," as if right out of your brain.

Off-the-Wall

That new talk-show host is definitely off-the-wall.

Meaning: shocking; very unusual

Origin: In handball, racquetball, and squash, a player hits the ball against the wall. When it comes off the wall, you don't always know where it's headed or what it's going to do. Some word experts think that's how this new expression, which describes unpredictable people or odd behavior, may have been thought up.

Off Your Rocker

"My boss is off his rocker. He wants me to be at work early the morning after the dance."

Meaning: crazy; silly; foolish; not thinking correctly   ⇨

Origin: People have been using this phrase since the mid-1800s. "Rocker" in this idiom refers to a rocking chair, and there are at least two theories about how being "off your rocker" came to mean "crazy." If you fell off your rocking chair, it was a sign of being mentally unstable. "Rockers" are also the two curved pieces upon which the chair rocks. A rocking chair with a missing rocker moves strangely, like a person whose thinking is mixed-up. Other expressions with similar meanings are "off your nut" and "off your trolley."

Old Hat

Let's try a new place for our next vacation. Dooley's Dude Ranch is so old hat.

Meaning: out-of-date; not new; too familiar; uninteresting

Origin: In the late 19th and early 20th centuries, when this phrase became popular, men and women wore hats much more than they do today. Most people wanted to keep up with the latest styles, and an old hat was no longer fashionable.

Old Wives' Tale

"Wearing garlic around your neck won't scare off evil. That's just an old wives' tale."

Meaning: a superstition; a belief or practice not based on fact

Origin: This idiom has a long history. Plato, a famous Greek philosopher who lived around 300 B.C., first used this phrase. In the 1300s it appeared in English. Then Erasmus, a Dutch scholar, put it in his writings in the 1500s. The "old wives" in this idiom refer to people during the olden days who gave advice based on superstitions. Some examples of these "tales" are "feed a cold and starve a fever," "don't touch a frog or you'll get warts," and "it's bad luck to walk under a ladder."

On a Shoestring

They tried to start a school band on a shoestring.

Meaning: on a strict budget; with or using very little money

Origin: No one today is quite sure about the origin of this idiom, although we know it started in America in the late 1800s. A "shoestring" is what we call a shoelace today. Perhaps the writer who first used this expression was comparing a tiny amount of money with a piece of string like a shoelace.

On Cloud Nine

"Frances is on cloud nine since being named Junior Scientist of the Year."

Meaning: blissfully happy; joyous

Origin: Though this saying comes from the late 19th century, nine has been a mystical number for thousands of years, back to the time of the ancient Greeks. The saying originally was "on cloud seven," probably coming from "seventh heaven," the highest of the heavens in Jewish religious literature. Nine was then substituted, perhaps because it is a sacred Christian number. This is because three is a trinity and represents perfect unity, and nine is a trinity of trinities (3 x 3). Other idioms that express great joy also suggest being up high: "on top of the world" (see page 136), "walking on air" (see page 202), and so on.

On Pins and Needles

"I was on pins and needles until I got the phone call that the plane had landed safely."

Meaning: waiting anxiously for something; extremely nervous; in great suspense

Origin: This saying was first used in the late 1800s. When you're waiting nervously for something to happen, you sometimes feel as if you can't sit still—like needles or pins are sticking you. A writer once said it was like being "on pins and needles," and the phrase stuck. Other expressions of nervousness are "butterflies in the stomach" (see page 24) and "on tenterhooks" (see page 132).

On Someone's Case

"His girlfriend was on his case because he started smoking again."

Meaning: to nag, find fault with, badger or scold someone constantly about his or her business, situation, circumstances

Origin: In this popular African-American idiom, "case" means your business or current situation in life. You often hear or read this expression either as a complaint that someone is on your case about something, or as a demand that someone get off your case about something.

On Tenterhooks

"Steven waited on tenterhooks to see if he would win the award."

Meaning: uncertain, anxious, very tense; in painful suspense about how something will turn out

Origin: In the mid-1700s, when this saying originated, a tenter was a frame for stretching newly woven cloth. The "tenterhook" was a hook or bent nail that held the cloth to the tenter. At that time a person who was worried sick not knowing the outcome of a situation was said to be "on tenters," meaning that their emotions were stretched out tensely. Later the phrase became "on tenterhooks," which expressed even sharper and more intense feeling.

On the Ball

Mr. Hsu hired me because he thinks I'm really on the ball.

Meaning: alert; effective; skillful; knowledgeable

Origin: This saying originated with British football—what we call soccer. It could also be said that a person is "on top of things." Also, in the all-American sport of baseball, a pitcher who was able to get something "on the ball" (like great speed) would be more likely to win the game. As ball games, including basketball, became more popular, so did this expression.

On the Cuff

"Cosmo couldn't pay his bill, so he asked the owner to put it on the cuff."

Meaning: on credit; to be paid later

Origin: This expression probably came from the days when bartenders in old saloons wore stiff cuffs that detached from the end of their shirt sleeves. When customers wanted to pay for their drinks at a later date, the bartender often wrote the charges down on his cuffs. There is another, similar idiom, "off the cuff," that has a totally different meaning: to speak about or do something freely without thinking about it first.

On the Double

The coach told the players to get onto the field on the double.

Meaning: very quickly; immediately; at a fast pace

Origin: This is an old army command. When the person in charge wanted the soldiers to march twice as fast as normal, he'd holler, "On the double!" which meant to double the speed. Today, anyone can use this expression when he or she wants someone to hurry up.

On the Fence

"Are you for or against the new honor code, or are you still on the fence?"

Meaning: neutral; undecided; not choosing one way or the other

Origin: This popular expression from the early 1800s makes you think of a person actually sitting on a fence, body right in the middle, not completely on one side or the other, with one leg dangling over each side. In the same way, if a person straddles an issue without committing himself or herself, that's a person "on the fence."

On the Fritz

We can't watch the game at my house because my TV is on the fritz.

Meaning: broken; out of order; not working

Origin: Though this expression is a recent one (the early 1900s), nobody today is quite sure how it got started. One word expert gave the following possible explanation. During World War I, a degrading term for a German soldier was "Fritz," a common German name (short for Friedrich). Something not working or ruined could be compared to the defeated Germans.

On the Horns of a Dilemma

"Jose liked both girls who asked him to the dance, and he didn't want to hurt either. He was on the horns of a dilemma."

Meaning: having to choose between two undesirable courses of action or unpleasant things.

Origin: A bull can be a fierce animal, and nobody wants to be stuck on the sharp points of a bull's horns. But you feel that you're in that position if you are forced to decide between two possibly dangerous choices. A similar saying was used by people in the Middle Ages and by the Dutch scholar Erasmus around the year 1500. In medieval times a "dilemma" was a way of arguing in which one of two statements must be proved to be true.

On the Hot Seat

"Mike was caught eating a candy bar at the weight loser's class—now he's really on the hot seat."

Meaning: in a difficult or uncomfortable position and subject to a lot of unpleasant questions and personal attacks

Origin: The "hot seat" in this expression refers to the electric chair. But you can be on—or in—the hot seat in a freezing cold room if you've been accused of doing something bad, or you've been caught in an embarrassing situation and people are questioning and criticizing you.

On the Rocks

"I need a loan because my dog-walking business is on the rocks."

Meaning: financially ruined or wrecked; near disaster; finished

Origin: An unfortunate ship that has run aground and is on the rocks will eventually sink. In the 1800s the phrase "on the rocks" (meaning headed for disaster) was expanded to describe many areas of life, not just ships at sea. Note: There's also a totally different meaning for this saying. A person can order a drink "on the rocks." In this case, "rocks" mean ice cubes.

On the Ropes

"Last summer, my ice cream store did a lot of business, but now, in the middle of winter, it's on the ropes."

Meaning: almost failing; on the verge of collapse; nearly ruined

Origin: This phrase was first used in the 1800s and referred to boxers who were almost knocked out. They hung onto the ropes around the boxing ring so they wouldn't totally collapse. Later the saying was expanded to include any person, business, or situation that was in great difficulty or nearly ruined.

On the Spur of the Moment

On the spur of the moment, I rode my bike fifteen miles for a slice of my favorite pecan pie.

Meaning: suddenly; acting without thinking about it first; impulsively

Origin: In the early 1800s, when this idiom was first being used, many people rode horses to get where they were going. Riders often wore short, spiked wheels, called spurs, on the heels of their boots. When they wanted to urge a horse to go faster, they pressed the spurs against its body. If an opportunity is like a spur that gets a person to do something impulsively without waiting, you can easily see how "on the spur of the moment" originated. Now, of course, it relates to any sudden decision to act and has nothing to do with horses.

On the Warpath

"Mr. Ozawa is on the warpath because his car broke down again."

Meaning: in a very angry mood; infuriated

Origin: This phrase is from the mid-1800s and originally referred to Native Americans who were often at war with settlers or other tribes about land rights. The expression meant "going to war." By the end of the 19th century, the meaning had grown to mean being in a rage about anything.

On Top of the World

When Grandpa's girlfriend said that she'd marry him, he was on top of the world.

Meaning: feeling extremely happy

Origin: Many writers have used this famous expression since the early 1900s with the verb "sitting." "Down" has always suggested downhearted feelings such as sadness and depression (see "down in the dumps," page 48). But being "up" or "on top" has meant emotions such as delight and joy (see "walking on air," page 202, and "on cloud nine," page 131). "The world" represents everything, such as your life, your job, and your family. So, if you're sitting "on top of the world," you're overjoyed because of good health, success, and so on.

Once in a Blue Moon

"The teacher is tough, but once in a blue moon she doesn't give us homework."

Meaning: almost never; very seldom; hardly ever

Origin: On some nights when the bright part of the moon is a crescent, some people say the other part has a bluish color to it. This "blue moon" is rare. A similar expression was first used in the early 1500s and has been popular ever since.

One Good Turn Deserves Another

"I helped Jill fix her flat tire, and she gave me a ride. One good turn deserves another."

Meaning: one good deed should be paid back with another

Origin: This is an adage, a general truth that people have come to accept over many years. It dates as far back as the early 1400s and means that if you receive help from someone, it's only fair and proper that you help that person in return. The meaning of "turn" here is a deed or action. The same idea, but in a negative sense, appears in the idiom "eye for an eye and a tooth for a tooth" (see page 58).

One-Horse Town

"They got fed up with the noisy, crowded city, so they moved to a one-horse town out West."

Meaning: a place with few comforts and activities; a dull rural town

Origin: This expression was first used in the 1850s when there were more horses than people in some American towns. If a town had only one horse, it must have been really small, with very little happening. This exaggerated saying became popular even though it is insulting. Now it can describe any business or project that's considered rather minor or dull.

One-Track Mind

Paul has a one-track mind. All he ever thinks about is football, football, football.

Meaning: always thinking about only one subject

Origin: Most railroads have at least two tracks so trains can go in different directions without crashing into one another. However, on a single-track railroad line, train traffic can move in only one direction at a time.

Open a Can of Worms

"If you mention my report card to my mother, you'll open a can of worms.

Meaning: to cause trouble; to set unpleasant events in motion

Origin: A can of worms might be fine to open if you are by the banks of a river on a summer's day getting ready to fish. But you wouldn't want to open it anywhere else; the situation might cause a lot of trouble! In this expression, "worms" are difficult or delicate issues. A related idiom is "let sleeping dogs lie" (see page 111).

Other Side of the Coin

"The new building is wonderful, but on the other side of the coin, it cost $10 million."

Meaning: opposite side or point of view

Origin: This metaphor has been around since the beginning of the 20th century and is widely used. Every coin has two sides, but you can see only one side at a time. Like a coin, every issue has more than one side to it. You have to know the "other side of the coin" to get the full story.

Out in Left Field

Mary's suggestion, a "dress as your favorite vegetable" party, was way out in left field.

Meaning: unusual; crazy; totally wrong

Origin: Baseball became a popular sport in the United States in the 20th century, and this expression is based on one of the field positions. Left field is a long way from home plate and is one of the farthest outfield positions to which fewer balls are hit. If home plate is called "home" because it's a safe place where a player starts out from and hopes to come back to, then "left field" means something far from what's considered normal. It's really weird!

Out in the Boondocks

She lives way out in the boondocks.

Meaning: in remote places; in rural regions; in sparsely populated areas

Origin: Tagalogs are native Filipinos who live in or near Manila, the capital city of the Philippines. In the Tagalog language, *bundok* means "mountain." The United States military forces stationed in the area of the Philippines in the first half of the 20th century extended the meaning of the word from mountain to any place that is far from heavily populated centers. Today, the saying is sometimes shortened to "in the boonies."

Out Like a Light

"Given a strong anesthetic, the patient was out like a light."

Meaning: fast asleep; suddenly unconscious

Origin: In America in the 20th century, when the wonders of electricity spread across the land, people could turn on and shut off lights with just a flick of a switch. By the middle of the century, "out like a light" was a way of saying that a person had fallen asleep very quickly or had been knocked out or drugged into unconsciousness in a matter of seconds.

Out of Here

"Just one more slice of cake and I'm out of here."

Meaning: good-bye; I'm going; I'm leaving

Origin: This catchy, modern African-American saying means just what it says.

Out of Sight, Out of Mind

"She thought she'd miss her boyfriend when he went away, but it was out of sight, out of mind."

Meaning: if you don't see something for a long time, you'll eventually stop thinking about it

Origin: Homer, an ancient Greek poet, used this proverb in his famous epic the *Odyssey* in about 850 B.C. A similar saying was popular in English

⇨

as early as the 1200s. The image is clear: what is missing from your view will soon be missing from your thoughts. The expression "absence makes the heart grow fonder" states the opposite idea.

Out of the Clear Blue Sky

Out of the clear blue sky, he asked her to marry him.

Meaning: suddenly and without any warning; totally unexpectedly

Origin: This late 19th-century expression is related to another saying, "a bolt from the blue" (see page 18). A bolt of lightning or sudden shower from a clear, blue sky would be unexpected. Sometimes this idiom is shortened to "out of the blue."

Out of the Frying Pan and into the Fire

"First you were late. Now, you spilled glue all over the teacher's desk. You've jumped out of the frying pan and into the fire."

Meaning: from a bad situation into one that is worse

Origin: This proverb, popular in many languages, was used in English in the early 1500s. A piece of food being fried in a pan is hot enough, but falling out of the frying pan and into the fire is even worse!

Out of the Mouths of Babes

"The four-year-old said, 'Aunt Roslyn, your dress is as pretty as a garden.' Out of the mouths of babes, you know."

Meaning: children can unexpectedly say very intelligent things

Origin: The full version of this saying is something like "out of the mouths of babes come smart ideas," but you don't have to say the whole thing for people to get the idea. Similar expressions originated in the Bible.

Out of the Woods

"The doctor says Bob's condition has improved slightly,
but he's not out of the woods yet."

Meaning: safe from trouble or danger

Origin: For centuries, at least back to ancient Roman times, people thought of the woods as a dark, mysterious, possibly dangerous place. If you were stuck in the woods, you could be in trouble. But if you got "out of the woods," you were safe. This expression can be used to mean being past any kind of critical phase in a risky situation or getting free of danger or trouble.

Out on a Limb

"The mayor went out on a limb when he opposed the new
sports center."

Meaning: taking a chance; in a dangerous position from which it is hard to withdraw or change

Origin: This American saying dates from the late 1800s, when hunting animals in the woods was a more common activity than it is today. It probably referred to a hunted animal that climbed a tree and got itself stranded out on a limb where it could easily be shot. Later the idiom grew to describe any person who takes a risk that might lead to trouble.

Over a Barrel

Jack is really over a barrel since he lost the only copy
of the book he needed for his report.

Meaning: helpless; in someone's power; at a disadvantage

Origin: There are a couple of possible explanations for this old idiom. One is that a person rescued from drowning was often laid over a barrel to help empty his or her lungs of water. The other is that a person about to be flogged, or whipped for a crime, was often tied over a barrel to hold him down.

Over the Hill

"A ninety-two-year-old man finished the marathon and proved he wasn't over the hill yet."

Meaning: past one's prime; unable to function as one used to; too old

Origin: Since at least the middle of the 20th century, writers have made comparisons between living your life and climbing a hill or mountain. When you're young and full of energy, you climb up the hill and head for the top. After that, as you come upon middle and old age, your body slows and you go down the hill, no longer able to do all the things you could do before. You're "over (the top of) the hill." But some old-timers would say, "I'd rather be over the hill than under it."

Over Your Head

I warned Charles that he was in over his head, but he wouldn't stop.

Meaning: a risky situation that will lead to certain failure; beyond your ability to understand something

Origin: This widely used expression has two meanings. One is that if you invest more money than you can afford in a risky business venture, then you're in "over your head" and probably on the road to financial disaster. In this case, you should try to "keep your head above water" (see page 104). The other meaning is that if a person tells a joke or makes a remark that you don't understand, it goes "over your head" rather than into your brain.

Par for the Course

"Mr. Hernandez gave me a 'C.' The way he's been grading lately, that's about par for the course."

Meaning: just what was expected; normal; typical

Origin: In the 1920s this expression, which came from golf, was broadened to include other activities in life. In golf, "par" is the number of golf strokes it usually takes for a golf expert to play a course. That's how "par for the course" came to mean a typical or expected result. It usually has a slightly negative tone to it: "It took me three hours to get home in this blizzard, about par for the course." Related expressions are "up to par" (satisfactory) and "below par" (unsatisfactory).

Pass the Buck

You've got to make the decision yourself. You can't pass the buck on this one.

Meaning: to pass on or make another person accept responsibility or blame for something one does not want to accept for his or her own

Origin: In a 19th-century American poker game, "buck" was a piece of buckshot (a shotgun pellet) or a pocketknife with a buckhorn handle. It was passed to you if you were the next dealer. By 1900, "passing the buck" meant shifting responsibility for something to another person. In 1949 President Harry Truman put a sign on his desk that read "The Buck Stops Here." That meant that he was accepting personal responsibility for all decisions that needed to be made and all actions that needed to be taken. He wasn't going to direct his problems to anybody else.

Pass the Hat

"I need money for the amusement park. I may just have to pass the hat."

Meaning: to ask for contributions; to beg

Origin: At one time, hats were passed around at entertainment events by people asking for money. The custom might have originated with street minstrels who entertained people and then requested payment. And a hat is an excellent container in which to collect money. A related expression is "hat in hand" (see page 87).

Pay through the Nose

"In that restaurant, you'll pay through the nose for a meal."

Meaning: to pay too much for something

Origin: Here's an idiom from the 1600s. "Rhino" was once a slang word for money, but originally it was the Greek word for nose. The two words are similar in sound and their meanings might have come together to make this expression. Another possibility comes from Danish authorities charging Irish people a poll tax in the 9th century and cutting off or slitting the noses of those who failed to pay their taxes. There's also a gambling origin tied to "bleeding" a player—duping him to lose all his money. Now, if you "pay through the nose," you'd be paying an extremely expensive price for something. A related body-part saying is "pay an arm and a leg."

Pen Is Mightier than the Sword

"I'd rather be a writer than a general because the pen is mightier than the sword."

Meaning: writing is more powerful than fighting

Origin: This famous saying was first used in the 1600s. It started out as "the pen is worse than the sword." A pen and a sword have certain characteristics in common. Both are thin, pointed, and handheld. But history has shown that writers and statesmen using their pens have often had a greater effect on the course of events than military leaders and conquerors wielding swords. Think of the Magna Carta, the Declaration of Independence, and other important writings that have changed the course of history more than wars have.

Penny for Your Thoughts

You seem so serious. A penny for your thoughts.

Meaning: What are you thinking? Tell me what is on your mind.

Origin: Early in the 1500s, when people first started using this expression, a penny was worth more than it is today. So if you offered a penny to a person who was either thinking or daydreaming, you'd be offering a lot to know what was going on in his or her mind.

Penny-Wise and Pound-Foolish

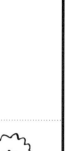

"That was penny-wise and pound-foolish. You saved a dollar in car fare when you walked all the way home, but now you need new sneakers."

Meaning: careful in small matters but careless about important things; saving small amounts of money while wasting large amounts

Origin: This was a well-known proverb by the early 1600s in England, where a pound is a unit of money. A penny was always worth much less than a pound. So the expression meant you were smart about things that were small and careless about things that were big.

People Who Live in Glass Houses Shouldn't Throw Stones

He complained about her driving, but he's already had two accidents. People who live in glass houses shouldn't throw stones.

Meaning: you should not criticize others if you are just as bad as they are

Origin: This saying became popular in the 1300s during the time of the English poet Geoffrey Chaucer, who used it in one of his books. If you lived in a glass house, you'd better hope that no one would throw stones at it! You should not judge other people if you have the same faults as they do.

Pie in the Sky

"Consuela thinks that if she goes to Washington, she'll meet the President and tell him her ideas. What a pie-in-the-sky idea!"

Meaning: something not possible; an unrealistic hope

Origin: In 1906 an American union organizer wrote a song called "The Preacher and the Slave" that had the words:

> Work and pray,
> Live on the hay,
> You'll get pie in the sky when you die!
> (That's a lie.)

"Pie" meant decent working conditions and good wages. Union workers wanted those things while they were alive, not after they died. The song was popular, and the phrase "pie in the sky" came to mean promised pleasures that probably won't come true, or rewards that are given after you die.

P

Piece of Cake

"Don't worry. Skateboarding down this hill is a piece of cake."

Meaning: an especially easy and pleasant task

Origin: This phrase could have come from an African-American dance contest in the mid-19th century. Contestants made up complex strutting movements, usually with high steps, and the winner won a cake. The dance was called the cakewalk, and the expression "that takes the cake" came from it. A related expression is "easy as pie."

Play Both Ends against the Middle

Zack got the other two candidates to call each other names, and he got elected. How's that for playing both ends against the middle.

Meaning: to pit two opponents against each other in such a way as to benefit yourself; to use each of two sides for your own purpose

Origin: In the 1800s there was a popular card game in America called faro, in which the dealer allowed a double bet by a player. The phrase was later applied to dishonestly using two opposing sides for one's selfish purposes.

Play Cat and Mouse

"Sherlock Holmes was toying with the suspect, playing cat and mouse with him."

Meaning: to fool or tease someone by pretending to let her or him go free and then catching her or him again

Origin: Cats are known for teasing mice by pretending to let them go and then grabbing them again. This game of capture and release might be repeated several times. Someone created the phrase "play cat and mouse" to suggest that human beings sometimes do the same thing: fool someone into thinking they're safe, and then pouncing. It also means to tease by keeping someone uninformed.

Play Fast and Loose

"You told Linda you'd help her, but then you didn't show up. You shouldn't play fast and loose with your friends."

Meaning: to do whatever pleases you without caring about what will happen to others; to be undependable and careless; to act irresponsibly

Origin: This saying might have come from a 14th-century game in which tricksters cheated people at country fairs by challenging them to perform impossible tricks and then taking their money when they couldn't. The game involved loops in a piece of string or folds in a belt. In the late 1500s William Shakespeare used this phrase in some of his plays. People who "play fast and loose" promise to do one thing and then do another.

Play Second Fiddle

"Why should Marianne play second fiddle to him? She's as smart as he is."

Meaning: to be a follower; to be in an inferior position

Origin: In an orchestra, there are the roles of first violin (or fiddle) and second fiddle. The person who plays "first violin" is supposed to be the most important musician in an orchestra. So, since at least the middle 1700s, when this saying was first used, "playing second fiddle" has meant to act the smaller part or be in a lower position rather than to be the leader.

Play the Field

I don't plan to date just one man. I'm going to play the field.

Meaning: to have many sweethearts or dates without going steady or committing yourself to one person

Origin: During the 19th century, gamblers who wanted to increase their chances of winning money at a horse race bet on every horse except the favorite. This was called "playing the field" (of horses). Later the phrase was extended to other areas of life, especially dating.

Play with Fire

"Threatening the bully in the neighborhood is really playing with fire."

Meaning: to take an unnecessary and dangerous risk; to court danger

Origin: This expression has been commonly used for hundreds of years, at least since the late 1500s. The metaphor is clear: If you're being irresponsible about something dangerous and inviting disaster, it's like playing with fire. You're taking a big risk.

Point of No Return

We can't cancel the show now. We've reserved the theater and sold tickets. We've reached the point of no return.

Meaning: the position or time after which it is impossible to go back, change your mind, or do something different

Origin: During World War II, pilots knew that they had only enough fuel to fly a certain number of miles. The point when they would reach the crucial mark was called the point of no return. If they continued to fly on, they would not have enough fuel to return to their home base.

Poor as a Church Mouse

"The Richards used to be wealthy, but after the stock market crash in 1987, they were as poor as church mice."

Meaning: very poor; poverty-stricken

Origin: This simile first appeared in English in the 17th century. Originally it was "hungry as a church mouse" because a mouse that was so unlucky as to live in a church would find no food there. Churches in the 1600s had no kitchens to cook meals and no pantries to store food. A smart mouse would take up residence in the cellar of a house, restaurant, or grocery store. As years went by, "hungry" was changed to "poor," and the idiom became popular in many countries.

Pot Calling the Kettle Black

For you to say that I can't throw a ball is like the pot calling the kettle black. You're a terrible pitcher!

Meaning: the person criticizing another person's faults is guilty of the same faults himself or herself

Origin: The theory about the origin of this idiom goes back to the early 1600s. It suggests that a pot and a kettle both got black from standing too long over an open fire. The pot couldn't fault the kettle for being blackened by smoke because the pot was the same color. In the same way, you can't criticize a person for something if the fault is one of yours, too. A similar idea is contained in the saying "People who live in glass houses shouldn't throw stones" (see page 145).

Pour Oil on Troubled Waters

"My brothers were having a terrible fight in the car, but my mother poured oil on troubled waters by saying they were both right."

Meaning: to calm an angry quarrel; to have a soothing effect through tact or skill in dealing with people

Origin: As early as A.D. 731 this expression referred to the belief that if you poured oil on rough, stormy ocean waves, it would calm them. Now it means to smooth over a stormy or disturbed situation of any kind on land or sea.

Power behind the Throne

"The president's wife had so much influence on him that people knew she was the real power behind the throne."

Meaning: the actual, but unrecognized, person in charge

Origin: This saying was being used in England by the 1770s. "Throne" does not always stand for a royal position. It could mean the office of any leader. If someone else is telling the leader what to do, he or she could be called the "power behind the throne."

Proof of the Pudding Is in the Eating

"The car looks gorgeous, but the only way to know how it runs is to test drive it. The proof of the pudding is in the eating."

Meaning: success is measured by the final result

Origin: This old proverb has been enormously popular since at least the 1600s, especially with British writers. The only way to know if a pudding is good and has turned out right is to taste it.

Pull a Fast One

"My sister pulled a fast one. She asked me to hold the brush. Then she left, and I had to finish painting the room."

Meaning: to deceive; to mastermind a trick or deception

Origin: This expression originated in the English sport of cricket, and meant to bowl a fast ball. It probably became popular in the United States either in reference to a fast shuffle of cards or to the fastball in baseball, which usually comes when you're not expecting it.

Pull a Rabbit Out of a Hat

We were hungry, but he found some cookies in his bag. It was like pulling a rabbit out of a hat.

Meaning: to produce something that is needed as if by magic; to unexpectedly find a solution to a problem

Origin: The magician's trick of pulling a live rabbit out of an empty top hat is very old, but this expression is relatively new (from about the 1930s). The meaning has been transferred from the specific (a magic trick) to the general (producing by surprise the answer to a difficulty). Sometimes this idiom is shortened, as in, "We didn't think we had a jack to fix the flat tire, but he just pulled one out of a hat."

Pull No Punches

"Tell me what you thought of my acting. Don't pull any punches."

Meaning: to hit as hard as possible; to attack with full force; to be perfectly honest; to not hold back

Origin: This saying came originally from the sport of boxing. If a fighter pulled back on a punch, he held back, didn't hit as hard as he could, and landed a soft blow. By the 1930s this expression was being used about all sorts of activities. If you pulled your punches, you were careful not to hurt anybody. If you pulled no punches, you were completely honest, even if it might hurt someone's feelings.

Pull Out All the Stops

Tonight I'm pulling out all the stops: candlelight dinner, violin music, champagne, the works! Then I'll ask her to marry me.

Meaning: to do everything possible to succeed; to do something as enthusiastically as you can

Origin: This saying comes from the second half of the 19th century and refers to the workings of big organs. Church organs had many pipes that an organist played by pulling out knobs called stops. If you pulled out all the stops, you got the fullest, loudest, most ear-filling sound possible. That idea was carried over to other activities in life where one goes all out to succeed or enjoy an activity.

Pull Strings

"The movie is sold out, but since your uncle runs the theater, maybe you could pull strings and get us tickets."

Meaning: to exert behind-the-scenes influence; to secretly control others from a distance as if they were puppets

Origin: Marionettes (string puppets) have been used to entertain people for centuries. A puppeteer, out of the sight of the audience, pulls the strings that make the puppets move.

P

Pull the Rug Out from Under You

I asked Marcus to be my campaign manager, but he decided to support someone else and pulled the rug right out from under me.

Meaning: to unexpectedly withdraw support; to suddenly place somebody at a disadvantage; to ruin someone's plans, hopes, or dreams

Origin: An American writer in the middle of the 20th century imagined a person standing on a rug, and then, all of a sudden, the rug pulled right out from under him or her. The person would be hurt or at a disadvantage lying on the floor. The writer applied that image to destroying someone's expectations or activities.

Pull the Wool Over Your Eyes

"Jacob tried to pull the wool over Ms. Jarvis's eyes by saying his dog had eaten his homework."

Meaning: to fool, deceive, or trick someone

Origin: In 19th-century Europe many men wore wigs made of wool. In British courts today, some lawyers and judges still wear them. If you pulled the wig over a person's eyes, he or she couldn't see what was happening and could easily be tricked. It was said that if a clever lawyer fooled a judge, he was "pulling the wool" over the judge's eyes. Now, we use this expression to describe any act of cheating or trickery.

Pull Up Stakes

"After I finish this project, I'm pulling up stakes and moving to New Hampshire."

Meaning: to leave your home, job, or country and move to another location looking for something better

Origin: This has been a well-used saying since at least the 17th century. Stakes (pointed pieces of wood) were often driven into the ground as markers to show the boundaries of an area of land. When you went out and pulled up the stakes, it often meant you were moving to a new location. This expression now refers to making a big move in one's life. When a circus left one town for another, the stakes that held the circus tents were pulled up, too.

Pull Your Leg

Oh, don't get so annoyed at them for teasing you. They're just pulling your leg.

Meaning: to tease or fool someone; to jokingly try to lie to somebody

Origin: By the late 1800s people sometimes tripped other people by catching their legs with a cane or running a string across the sidewalk. Sometimes it was just for fun; at other times robbers did it to steal from the victim after he or she had fallen.

Pull Yourself Together

"Calm down, pull yourself together, and fly this plane!"

Meaning: to regain control over one's emotions and become calm after being very upset

Origin: There are many modern idioms that relate to becoming emotionally upset: "blowing one's top," "breaking down," "falling apart," "going to pieces," "losing one's head," and so on. All of them suggest that you lose control of your feelings. So, when people regain their composure and are calm again, they have pulled themselves together.

Put All Your Eggs into One Basket

"Keith used all his savings to start a fishing business, but I told him not to put all his eggs into one basket."

Meaning: to risk everything you have at once on a single idea or plan; to commit all your resources at one time

Origin: The idea for this idiom goes back to the 1600s when someone realized that if you put all your eggs into one basket and then dropped that basket, all your eggs would be smashed at once. Figuratively speaking, if you place all of your hopes and efforts on just one thing, you might lose everything.

Put Your Best Foot Forward

"When you go in for your interview, try to put your best foot forward."

Meaning: to make the best attempt possible; to do your best to make the greatest impression you can

Origin: Although this saying has been around since at least 1500, no one today is quite sure how it originated. One possibility is that if one leg of your pants is torn or dirty and you're meeting someone new, you'd put the good foot forward to make the best first impression.

Put Your Finger on Something

"Ann knew the Civil War had taken place in the 1800s, but she couldn't put her finger on the exact dates."

Meaning: to identify something precisely; to point out or describe exactly

Origin: This idiom is easy to imagine: If you can actually put your finger right onto something, then you know exactly where it is. If you can recall something exactly (name, date, or specific fact), then you're "putting your finger on it."

Put Your Foot Down

Max's mother put her foot down and demanded he be home by 10 P.M.

Meaning: to be firm or rigid about something

Origin: Versions of this expression started in the 1500s, but it became popular in the 1800s. Stomping your foot down to get someone's attention sometimes expresses a strong position or demand. If you state a rule and expect someone to obey it, you've "put your foot down."

Put Your Money where Your Mouth Is

"If you're so certain that you'll win the violin contest, why don't you put your money where your mouth is?"

Meaning: to be willing to bet on or invest your money in something you support or believe in

Origin: Since about 1930 people in the United States have been challenging other people with this expression. "Mouth" represents talk. "Money" means action or investing. It's a way of saying that you should back up your words with action, often a bet or an investment of money, to prove that you really believe what you're saying. A ruder version of this idea is "Put up or shut up."

Put Your Shoulder to the Wheel

Irving didn't give up when the work got hard. He put his shoulder to the wheel and finished.

Meaning: to make a great effort; to begin to work hard

Origin: This idiom first appeared in the 1600s. The writer who thought it up imagined a wagon stuck in mud. As the horse pulled, the driver would have to put his shoulder to one of the back wheels and push to get the wagon rolling again. Starting in the 1700s, the saying included any kind of hard labor necessary to accomplish a task.

Q.T.
(also QT and q.t.)

"She doesn't know about the surprise party, so keep it on the Q.T."

Meaning: quietly; secretly; without anyone knowing

Origin: Sometimes we abbreviate words by using their first and last letters. For example, the standard post office abbreviation for Maryland is MD, and for Kentucky, it's KY. In 1870 there was a popular ballad called "The Talkative Man from Poplar." In one of the lines the word "quiet" was shortened to "q.t." Some people think this abbreviation could have been used in earlier writings, but after 1870 "on the q.t." became a common phrase for "keep it quiet."

Quick on the Draw

"In math, she's always quick on the draw."

Meaning: ready, alert, and quick to respond or react; mentally fast; quick to grasp information; touchy, sensitive

Origin: In the American West of the mid-1800s many gunslingers prided themselves on how fast they could draw their pistols from their holsters and shoot. The idea of a "quick draw" caught on and was transferred to any kind of fast action, physical or mental, such as responding quickly, answering questions rapidly, or solving problems swiftly. Similar expressions are "quick on the trigger" and "quick on the uptake."

Quiet as a Mouse

Quiet as a mouse, she slipped back into her dormitory after hours.

Meaning: silent or still; making very little noise; saying nothing; hushed, subdued

Origin: There are many similes in English that use animal traits, such as "sly as a fox" and "wise as an owl." "Quiet as a mouse" goes back to the late 1500s. Mice are quiet little animals who scurry almost noiselessly in search of food, especially in the dark of night.

Rain Check

> The store had run out of the guitars that were on sale, so they gave us a rain check.

Meaning: a ticket stub allowing attendance at a future event in place of one that was canceled; a piece of paper from a store for buying a sold-out item at the sale price at a later date

Origin: Rain checks were first issued at baseball games in the 1800s, and that's when this phrase became popular. If the game was rained out, you took your rain check ticket and used it to get a ticket for a future game at no extra cost.

Raining Cats and Dogs

"It's raining cats and dogs, and our picnic is ruined."

Meaning: to rain very heavily; to pour

Origin: There are several theories about the origin of this popular idiom, which goes back at least to the middle 1700s in England. One comes from Norse mythology, in which dogs were associated with windy storms and cats were associated with rain. Also, in England in the 17th and 18th centuries, many cats and dogs drowned in floods caused by torrential rainstorms, and their bodies were found in the streets afterwards as if they had fallen from the sky with the rain.

Rain or Shine

"Kathy is going to her sister's wedding next Thursday, rain or shine."

Meaning: no matter what happens; whatever the weather is like

Origin: Since at least the early 1600s people have been using this expression to declare that some activity will definitely take place regardless of the weather or any other unpredictable circumstances, bad or good.

Raise an Eyebrow

"It raised quite a few eyebrows when Sara showed up with her hair dyed purple and green."

Meaning: to surprise or shock people by doing or saying something outrageous; to cause somebody to show disapproval in his or her facial expression

Origin: This fairly modern idiom represents what happens to a lot of people's faces when they see something that really startles them: They raise their eyebrows. This expression can suggest a person's emotional reaction to something surprising or shocking, even if it doesn't show on his or her face.

Raise Cain

He raised Cain when he realized he had been overcharged.

Meaning: to be very angry, complain loudly, and make trouble

Origin: Though this saying originated in the middle 1800s, it refers to the story in the Bible about wicked Cain, who killed his brother Abel. Cain's name became associated with wild behavior. If you get furious enough to cause a loud disturbance and make trouble, then you're "raising Cain." Related sayings are "kick up a fuss," "raise the devil," and "raise the roof."

Rally Round the Flag

"To show we still love our team, let's rally round the flag, even if they lose."

Meaning: to come together to show support, especially in bad times

Origin: General Andrew Jackson first used this phrase at the Battle of New Orleans in 1815 when he wanted his troops to come together ("rally") to fight the British Army in the War of 1812. The "flag" Jackson referred to was the U.S. flag, of course. (The United States won the war, and Jackson went on to become the seventh President of the country, 1829–37). Then the saying was included in the words to a song sung during the Civil War: "Yes, we'll rally round the flag, boys, we'll rally once again. Shouting the battle cry of freedom." Today people use the expression to show support for anyone or anything in any situation.

Rat Race

"Let's quit this rat race and backpack around the world."

Meaning: a fierce, unending, stressful competition in business or society

Origin: Rat racing isn't a sporting event. Rats do have a reputation for relentlessness, competitiveness, and speed. This expression's origin is a nautical phrase for a fierce tidal current; "rat" and "race" are forms of the French "ras," which means "tide-race." "Rat race" suggests a confusing, crowded, useless scramble for survival, and, unfortunately, many people use the phrase to describe their jobs and lives.

Rats Abandoning a Sinking Ship

Like rats abandoning a sinking ship, they switched to the other candidate when theirs began to lose.

Meaning: disloyal people who desert a failing enterprise before it's too late

Origin: This idiom has been known since at least the 1500s. There was an old superstition among sailors that if they saw rats jumping off a ship that was still tied up in port, that was an omen that the ship would end in disaster. We now use this phrase to describe cowardly, unfaithful human beings who forsake something or someone they once supported because they think bad times are coming.

Read Between the Lines

"When Mr. Allen said he'd find a good part for me, I knew he meant I didn't get the leading role. I can read between the lines."

Meaning: to discern the true, hidden meaning or fact in any document or action

Origin: There are forms of cryptography (secret-message writing) in which cryptographers have to read between the lines of writing or read every other line to decode the real meaning of a message. This idiom suggests that sometimes people write or talk in such a way that their true intentions are hidden. If you "read between the lines," you will figure out the true, unexpressed meaning in an action or document.

Read the Riot Act

> When I saw what my little sister had done to my stereo, I read her the riot act.

Meaning: to severely scold or warn someone

Origin: In 1714 the British Parliament passed what was called the Riot Act. It said if twelve or more people gathered "illegally, riotously, and tumultuously," a magistrate could command them to break up and leave just by reading the opening words of the Riot Act. If they didn't leave within an hour, they were guilty of breaking the law and were given a severe punishment. As the years went by, "reading someone the riot act" came to mean warning a person in the strongest possible terms of severe punishment if he or she did not stop a certain activity.

Real McCoy

"That is a fake antique. This one's the real McCoy."

Meaning: the genuine article; something of good quality, compared to others; not a fake or copy

Origin: There are two good possibilities as to this idiom's origin. One is a boxer in the late 1800s who called himself Kid McCoy. (His real name was Norman Selby.) He was a great fighter and so popular that other boxers started calling themselves Kid McCoy. So Mr. Selby had to bill himself as "the real McCoy." Other word experts trace this idiom to Elijah McCoy (1843–1929), an African-American inventor who was best known for inventing lubricating parts for steam engines.

Red-Carpet Treatment

"When the President arrived, he was given the red-carpet treatment."

Meaning: great respect and hospitality given to someone important; special treatment

Origin: There is an ancient custom of putting down a red carpet over which an important dignitary would walk when he or she arrived someplace. Even today, the red carpet is rolled out at public buildings to welcome important people. But if you welcome a person extravagantly, you're "rolling out the red carpet" even if you don't have a carpet at all.

Red Herring

"In the scavenger hunt, 'See the bee in the old oak tree,' was a false clue, a red herring to throw us off the trail."

Meaning: something deliberately misleading to divert your attention from the main subject; something irrelevant that confuses an issue

Origin: A red herring is a fish that has been pickled (preserved in vinegar and spices) in such a way that it turns reddish. It has a strong smell. Centuries ago it was used to teach hunting dogs to follow a trail. It was dragged on the ground and the dogs followed its scent. Later, people who hated hunting dragged a red herring across the path of the fox the dogs were chasing. The dogs would get confused, stop following the fox, and follow the smell of the herring. Sometimes escaping crooks also used red herrings to cover up their own scents so the bloodhounds couldn't find them. "Red herring" has been a popular idiom since the 19th century.

Red-Letter Day

My father said that the day I was born was a red-letter day for him.

Meaning: a day remembered as especially happy and significant

Origin: In medieval times, religious festivals, holidays, and saints' days were printed in red ink on church calendars. (The other days were in black.) The "red-letter days" were the really special ones. Any day remembered because it's particularly pleasant or important can be called a red-letter day no matter what color ink it's printed in on your calendar.

Red Tape

"Why can't the mayor just cut all the red tape and let us have a parade without a permit?"

Meaning: excessive formality and time-consuming, rigid adherence to rules and regulations

Origin: Red ribbon was once used by lawyers and government employees to tie up bundles of legal documents. Before any official business could be transacted, the red tape had to be cut. We use "red tape" to refer to any kind of trivial and needless delay caused by time-consuming, bureaucratic work and office routines in an organization.

Right off the Bat

> All she said was, "How are you?" and right off the bat he told her all his troubles.

Meaning: immediately, spontaneously, and without delay

Origin: This saying comes from the game of baseball in the late 1800s. As soon as a ball is hit by a bat, it flies away instantly, without a second's delay.

Ring a Bell

"I don't remember her face, but her name rings a bell."

Meaning: to sound familiar; to call something to mind; to stir a vague memory

Origin: This American idiom from the early 1900s suggests that there are many bells that ring to remind or instruct us to do things: doorbell (open the door), telephone bell (pick up the phone), school bell (come to class), toaster bell (take out the toast), clothes dryer bell (take out the clothes), and so on. So, if something such as a face, a name, a number, or a date "rings a bell," it causes you to remember something.

Rock the Boat

"Lauren and Ellis got along just fine until Ellis rocked the boat by lighting up a cigar."

Meaning: to make trouble and disrupt a stable situation; to risk spoiling a plan; to create a disturbance

Origin: Since the 1920s this saying has been popular in both the United States and England. Imagine you're in a small boat. Everything's peaceful. Suddenly, someone or something rocks the boat. The boat may capsize or even sink! People who "rock the boat" cause trouble wherever they are.

Roll with the Punches

"Try not to be too discouraged with your new job. Just roll with the punches awhile."

Meaning: to adjust to a difficult situation; to not let little annoyances bother you, in order to survive

Origin: Every good boxer knows how to take evasive action to avoid the full force of an opponent's blow: He rolls with the punches. If he can't duck the blow entirely, he shifts his body and moves it in the direction of the punch to soften the impact. This boxing lesson can be applied to any situation in life.

Rolling Stone Gathers No Moss

"He's moved three times in three years, so he doesn't have any furniture or close friends. A rolling stone gathers no moss."

Meaning: a person who is always on the move or who changes jobs often will not be able to save or keep much

Origin: This ancient proverb, which appears in many languages, was made more popular when Erasmus, the famous Dutch theologian and scholar, used it in 1523. Moss is a green plant that usually grows in patches on a stone if it remains in one place for a long time. If the stone rolls, no moss will grow on it. "A rolling stone gathers no moss" is a warning to restless wanderers that they had better settle down somewhere or they might not have much to show for themselves over time.

Rome Was not Built in a Day

Don't give up on your model for the Young Inventors contest. Rome wasn't built in a day.

Meaning: a difficult or important goal or task cannot be achieved quickly or all at once

Origin: Rome, the beautiful city on the Tiber River in Italy, was the capital of the Roman Empire. It took centuries for Rome to be built to its full glory. There's a lesson in that. If "Rome wasn't built in a day," then you should be willing to persevere when you're working on a project. Major accomplishments don't happen overnight. Two similar proverbs are, "where there's a will, there's a way" and "if at first you don't succeed, try, try again."

163

Rotten Apple Spoils the Barrel

A tiny group of kids starts fights in our school, and people think that one rotten apple spoils the barrel.

Meaning: one bad person or thing may spoil an entire group

Origin: Benjamin Franklin included this saying in his *Poor Richard's Almanack* in 1736, but it goes all the way back to the mid-1500s. It is true that if you allow one apple in a barrel to rot, it may rot the other apples. Rottenness sometimes spreads. This thought has been transferred to people. One dishonest individual in a group can sometimes corrupt others.

Round Peg in a Square Hole

"Although Matt got a job in an auto repair shop, he's a round peg in a square hole. He doesn't know how to fix cars."

Meaning: a person whose abilities, character, or personality are not suited to his or her position

Origin: This familiar saying has been used since at least 1800 to describe people who just don't fit the situations they're in. They don't have the skills, the knowledge, or maybe the temperament. Sometimes the words in this expression are switched to "square peg in a round hole."

Rub Elbows with Someone

"On her last vacation Samantha went to Hollywood, where she says she rubbed elbows with a lot of stars."

Meaning: to be in the same place with others; to associate with people

Origin: In England people say "rub shoulders," but since about the middle 1800s Americans say "rub elbows." No matter, because if you're close enough to anyone so that your elbows or shoulders touch, you're pretty close. People today often brag that they "rubbed elbows" with someone famous.

Rub the Wrong Way

"It certainly rubbed Mary Jane the wrong way when Mike asked her if she got her hair cut in a pet shop."

Meaning: to annoy and irritate someone; to handle someone insensitively

Origin: Since the mid-1800s people have been using this idiom to express the act of really irritating someone with something you said or did. This phrase may have originated from cleaning or preparing wood and making the mistake of going against its grain. Rubbing it the wrong way would make it rough and streaked. A related idiom is "against the grain" (see page 78).

Run Circles around Someone

"Isaac thinks he's a good math student, but Margaret could run circles around him."

Meaning: to easily do something far better than someone else

Origin: In the late 1800s the writer who made up this saying might have imagined two runners. One was so fast that he could actually run in circles ("rings") around his slower competitor and still win the race. Today if you can "run rings around" someone else, you're much better than he or she is in a skill.

Run off at the Mouth

Ms. Rosario was running off at the mouth again about the kids playing basketball in her backyard.

Meaning: to talk too much; to talk nonstop

Origin: This is a colorful, modern African-American expression. It calls to mind one definition of the verb "to run" that relates to water: to flow quickly. Imagine a flood of words gushing rapidly out of someone's mouth and you get the idea.

Salt of the Earth

"Sonia is considered the salt of the earth. She volunteers for any job."

Meaning: a person or group considered to be the finest, most admirable, and noble

Origin: For thousands of years salt has been one of the most valuable, useful, and desired things. At one time, Roman soldiers were paid part of their salaries in salt (see "worth your salt," page 208). The expression "salt of the earth" is even found in the Bible (Jesus' Sermon on the Mount, Matthew 5:13). It is a metaphor that describes the finest people on earth as being as significant as the extremely important commodity of salt.

Save for a Rainy Day

Ads from the bank keep advising people to save some money for a rainy day.

Meaning: to save for a time of need; to put something away for the future

Origin: Since the 16th century "rainy day" has meant a time of need, misfortune, hardship, and affliction. So if things are "sunny" for you now, don't waste everything you have. Put some away for a "rainy day" because circumstances may change.

Saved by the Bell

"My sister was just about to show everyone an embarrassing picture of me when I was saved by the bell. The lights went out."

Meaning: rescued at the last possible moment from an embarrassing or dangerous situation

Origin: If a boxer is being badly beaten or has been knocked down and the referee is counting to ten, the sound of the bell means he doesn't have to continue the fight. The round is over and he can rest for a little while. In the middle of the 20th century, this exclamation was transferred to any happy, last-minute rescue from a bad situation.

Saw Logs

I could hear Dad sawing logs on the living room couch.

Meaning: to snore, to breathe loudly through your nose while you're sleeping soundly

Origin: This is a sound-effect idiom. In the early 1900s a writer with a good ear for sounds was looking for an imaginative way to describe someone snoring with gusto. The sound of snoring reminded him of wood being sawed. Even today, cartoonists sometimes draw a picture of logs with a saw in them above the heads of sleeping people.

Scarce as Hen's Teeth

"During the holidays, seats on any flight were as scarce as hen's teeth."

Meaning: very, very rare or totally nonexistent

Origin: This 19th-century American expression—sometimes expressed as "scarcer than a hen's tooth"—comes right from the chicken coop, where hens are found. Hens don't have teeth. They grind up their food in their gizzards (stomachs). Since hen's teeth don't exist, what could be rarer than that?

Scrape the Bottom of the Barrel

"I rented the last car, and they really scraped the bottom of the barrel to find that one."

Meaning: to use whatever is left after the best have been taken; to be forced to use the remnants of something; to choose among the worst of something

Origin: Many things are stored in barrels, and the dregs sink to the bottom. So, if you need something urgently and most of it has already been taken, you have to scrape the bottom of the barrel to get whatever you can. This idiom applies to having to take the worst of something because there's nothing good left.

Scratch the Surface

"Doctors have only scratched the surface in finding the cure for this disease."

Meaning: to just begin to deal with a problem; to deal with only a very small part of a subject

Origin: This well-used saying comes from the 1800s. In farming, to prepare the soil for planting you have to dig deeply. In archaeology, to uncover ancient treasures you often have to dig deeply. If, in any area, you only "scratch the surface," you'd be doing the task superficially. By the 1900s, this saying was transferred to all areas of life.

Security Blanket

"My little brother took his old stuffed penguin to school. It was his security blanket."

Meaning: a person or a thing that an insecure individual holds onto for emotional comfort or psychological reassurance

Origin: Many young children cling to something (a blanket or favorite stuffed toy, for instance) because it makes them feel safe and gives them confidence. Charles M. Schulz, the American cartoonist who draws the popular comic strip "Peanuts," created a character named Linus who always drags around his "security blanket," a term that Schulz coined.

See Eye to Eye

My parents and I don't always see eye to eye about my allowance.

Meaning: to agree fully; to have the same opinion

Origin: This expression can be found in the Bible (Isaiah 52:8). Imagine two people, side by side, watching the same thing. Since they have the same view in mind, and since they're eye to eye (right next to each other), they will probably agree on what they're both experiencing. In the same way, people on opposite sides of the world can see "eye to eye" on an issue if they both think the same way about it.

Sell like Hotcakes

"The footballs autographed by the state champion were selling like hotcakes."

Meaning: to sell quickly, effortlessly, and in quantity

Origin: Today at carnivals, circuses, and amusement parks, people can buy hot dogs, hamburgers, and ice cream. In the late 1600s, however, hot cakes (pancakes) made on a griddle were the best-selling items at fairs, benefits, and events. By the middle of the 1800s the expression "selling like hot cakes" was transferred to any product that was being rapidly bought up by the public.

Set Your Teeth on Edge

When my grandfather listens to the governor talk about the economy, it sets his teeth on edge.

Meaning: to cause annoyance or discomfort to someone

Origin: You can find this saying in several places in the Bible. Have you ever bitten on a piece of tinfoil? Did someone ever scratch his or her fingernails on the chalkboard while you were close by? You probably felt a sharp, shuddering feeling that made you gnash your teeth together.

Settle an Old Score

"It took her two years, but Shirley finally settled an old score with Roger."

Meaning: to get back at; to get revenge for past wrongs

Origin: In 17th-century England, a bill was known as a "score." So if you settled your score, you paid what you owed on your back bills. This phrase is now applied to clearing up any problems with people, usually by getting even with them for bad things that they once did to you.

Shake a Leg

Shake a leg or you're going to miss the bus.

Meaning: to hurry up; to go faster; to speed up

Origin: This lively American expression from the late 1800s is an order to someone who is moving too slowly. When you remain still, your legs are motionless. So when somebody tells you to "shake a leg," that's a command to get going. This expression comes from the navy.

Shape Up or Ship Out

"After he dropped his third tray of food, the owner told the new waiter that he'd better shape up or ship out."

Meaning: to correct your behavior, improve your performance, do your job satisfactorily, or get out

Origin: This sharp command was first uttered in the United States Armed Forces during World War II. It meant that a soldier, sailor, or marine had better conform to regulations and perform his tasks well ("shape up") or he would be sent overseas to a combat zone ("ship out"). After the war the expression was extended to include any area that demanded improved performance—or else!

Shoe Is on the Other Foot

"Once you drove right by me in the rain and didn't stop. Now the shoe is on the other foot. I'm driving, you're walking."

Meaning: the situation now is the opposite of what it once was; places are reversed

Origin: In the mid-19th century this expression was "the boot is on the other leg." You'll probably be surprised to learn that until the 1800s, there were no left or right boots or shoes. You could put either one on either foot, and if you kept putting the same shoe on the same foot, eventually the shoe would conform to the shape of that foot. If one day you accidentally put the wrong shoe on the wrong foot, the situation would be the opposite of what it had been. In the same way, if the boss becomes an employee and the employee becomes the boss, then "the shoe is on the other foot." The conditions are reversed.

Shoot from the Hip

In the interview, Perry just shot from the hip and got himself into a lot of trouble.

Meaning: to speak or act without first thinking about the consequences

Origin: In the olden days of the Western gunfighters, it was quicker to shoot your revolver from the side of your hip as soon as you pulled it from the holster than it was to raise it higher and shoot. If you had a good aim, this method was fast and accurate. Later this idea was transferred to talking or acting aggressively, recklessly, and impulsively without thinking of the effect of your actions.

Shot in the Arm

"Mr. Reynolds was feeling pretty low in the hospital, but your card really gave him a shot in the arm."

Meaning: something that lifts your spirits, energy, and confidence

Origin: This 1900s idiom originated with drug use involving hypodermic needles. Then, the saying meant a short boost or false hope. A shot of medicine can make someone feel better. In the same way, anything that renews your spirits, gives you a boost, and inspires, stimulates, or encourages you is like a shot in the arm.

Show Must Go On

"The bride had planned a wedding outdoors, and even when it rained, she insisted that the show must go on."

Meaning: the proceedings must continue regardless of any catastrophe or difficulty; nothing can stop what has been planned

Origin: The idea that you shouldn't let anything interrupt your big plans no matter what misfortune happens originated among stage performers. William Shakespeare wrote "Play out the play" in one of his works, and it has been a tradition in show business to put on the performance even if a lead actor is sick or the scenery has fallen down. In the 20th century this theatrical determination was transferred to anything in life that has to take place, no matter what.

Show Your True Colors

"We thought Carl was a great guy until he showed his true colors by kicking his dog."

Meaning: to reveal what you are really like

Origin: For centuries ships have flown colorful flags to identify themselves. Sometimes a ship could fool an enemy by flying a false flag that looked friendly. That was called sailing "under false colors." Then, if the deceitful ship "showed its true colors," it hoisted its real flags and showed the enemy who it really was. In the same way, people who show their true colors today are exposing their real traits, qualities, and character.

Sick as a Dog

Janine can't come to class today. She's as sick as a dog.

Meaning: very sick; suffering miserably without an ailment

Origin: This popular simile dates from the 1500s or even earlier. Dogs are among the most popular animals in the world of idioms. Think of "a dog's life," "going to the dogs," "in the doghouse," "let sleeping dogs lie," "raining cats and dogs," "you can't teach an old dog new tricks," and so on. Since a dog is a common household pet that often eats things it shouldn't and gets sick, it's a natural choice for this idiom.

Sight for Sore Eyes

"Mel was lost in the woods and getting hungry. All of a sudden he saw a sight for sore eyes—a park ranger at a hot-dog stand."

Meaning: a most welcome, unexpected sight; a pleasant surprise

Origin: In the 1700s an imaginative writer wrote that a welcome sight could figuratively cure sore eyes. What made the eyes "sore"? Some painful, worrisome, or distressing situation, most likely. Today, if you're in some kind of trouble, and into your view comes someone or something that can help, that's a "sight for sore eyes."

Sing for Your Supper

"Dad said I'd have to sing for my supper: Before he'd take me to the tennis match, I had to finish my homework."

Meaning: to perform a service in return for something one needs or wants

Origin: Starting in medieval times, it was common for a wandering, hungry minstrel to arrive at an English tavern and offer to sing poetry in exchange for a meal. By the early 1600s "sing for your supper" meant doing a favor or some kind of work in order to earn something you needed or desired.

Sink or Swim

"I moved to a faraway city and had to sink or swim without my parent's help."

Meaning: to fail or succeed by one's own efforts without anyone's help or interference

Origin: If you fail at learning to swim, you'll sink, of course. If you succeed, you'll swim. A related idiom for managing to succeed is to "keep your head above water" (see page 104). There was also a cruel and bizarre old-time practice of throwing a person suspected of being a witch into deep water. The accused were usually women. If the woman sank (and drowned), she was innocent. If she floated, then the devil must have helped her and she was guilty. Geoffrey Chaucer, an English poet, used the phrase "float or sink" in his writings in the 1300s.

Sitting Duck

Don't stay by yourself in the school yard after school. You'll be a sitting duck for all the bullies.

Meaning: someone or something likely to be attacked and unable to put up a defense

Origin: A duck hunter knows that if a duck is sitting still, it's a much easier target than a duck in flight. By the first half of the 20th century, the phrase "sitting duck" was transferred to any person who was an easy mark for someone who wanted to cheat or do him or her harm.

S

Sitting Pretty

"Rosa finished her book report and now she's sitting pretty."

Meaning: to be in a lucky, superior, or advantageous position

Origin: This American colloquialism comes from the early 1900s. "Sitting" is a comfortable position and "pretty" is an adjective suggesting beauty or favor. To the person who made up this phrase, "sitting pretty" must have suggested an easy, favorable situation.

Six of One and a Half Dozen of the Other

I don't care if we eat Italian or Chinese food. To me, it's six of one and a half dozen of the other.

Meaning: one and the same; nothing to choose between; equal

Origin: Charles Dickens, an English novelist, used this phrase in one of his books in 1852, but it has been known since the early 1800s. Six equals a half dozen, no matter which way you say it. So we can use this expression to refer to two things that offer no real choice because there's no real difference between them.

Skate on Thin Ice

"You'll be skating on thin ice if you wake me up tonight."

Meaning: to take a big chance; to risk danger; to start out on a hazardous course of action

Origin: Sometimes foolish people skate on thin ice just for the thrill of it. They think if they skate really fast, the ice might not crack. We use this expression to refer to any risky situation you might get yourself into. You could be in danger of suffering serious consequences. (Sometimes this expression is shortened to just "on thin ice.")

Skeleton in Your Closet

"Lizzie was close to being elected until her opponent exposed the skeleton in her closet."

Meaning: a shameful and shocking secret that people try to keep hidden

Origin: Nobody today really knows where this expression came from, although many 19th-century British writers used it in their books. There is a story about a man who killed his rival and hid the body in his closet to keep the secret from his neighbors. Eventually, they found out he had a "skeleton in the closet."

Sky's the Limit

Order anything on the menu—the sky's the limit.

Meaning: there's no limit to what you can spend or how far you can go or what you can achieve

Origin: The idea of the sky being the limit goes back to at least the 1600s; even then people saw no limit to the sky. The exact wording of this idiom in English is from the 1900s. It might have been used in gambling to indicate that there was no limit to the size of a bet someone could make. Today, you can apply this description to many other situations in life.

Sleep on It

"The boss said he'd tell me tomorrow if I got the job or not. He had to sleep on it."

Meaning: to put off making a decision until at least the next day so that you can think about it overnight

Origin: For thousands of years people have wanted to have extra time to make up their minds about issues. In the early 1500s someone decided to call this process "sleeping on it," and the expression has been popular ever since.

Sling Hash

"To earn money for college, Laurie got a job slinging hash."

Meaning: to work as a waiter, waitress, or cook in a cheap, small restaurant serving inexpensive fast food

Origin: This saying from the mid-1800s describes a type of job. Waiters and waitresses in small diners, drive-ins, and fast-food restaurants didn't serve expensive, beautifully prepared meals. They would often quickly throw ("sling") plates of cheap food, such as browned meat, potatoes, and vegetables ("hash"), on the table. There are plenty of places today where servers are still slinging hash.

Slow on the Draw

Some of Albert Einstein's teachers thought he was a little slow on the draw.

Meaning: slow to understand or figure something out; slow to respond or react; not alert; not a deep thinker

Origin: In the American West of the 1800s you often had to be quick on the draw (get your pistol out of the holster fast) to stay out of trouble. If you drew your revolver slowly, you were a candidate for the undertaker. Eventually, the term "slow on the draw" was extended to include actions of the mind and not just the hand. Similar expressions are "slow off the mark" and "slow on the uptake."

Smell a Rat

"Although everything looked all right, the investigator smelled a rat."

Meaning: to be suspicious; to feel that something is wrong

Origin: Rats are among the most unpopular animals. When most people think of rats, they think of disgusting, wicked, horrible images. Cats have been sniffing out rats for thousands of years, and in the mid-1500s the phrase "smell a rat" was used for human beings who suspected ("smelled") that something illegal, evil, or sinful ("a rat") had taken place.

Smell like a Rose

"Even though Sam causes all the trouble, he comes up smelling like a rose."

Meaning: to look good in a bad situation; to avoid a damaged reputation when involved with corruption; to appear pure and innocent

Origin: Most people love the smell of roses, and there are many perfumes that try to capture their fragrance. The American writer who thought up this early 20th-century expression must have imagined someone who falls into something filthy such as a swamp and amazingly manages to come out smelling sweet.

Snake in the Grass

"What a snake in the grass he was! He was only pretending to be my friend."

Meaning: an unfaithful, untrustworthy, underhanded, and deceitful person; a traitor

Origin: For thousands of years people have feared and hated snakes—at least since 37 B.C., when the great Roman poet Virgil used this expression. A snake is often not out in the open where you can see it; it's hiding in the grass.

Snug as a Bug in a Rug

Grandma tucked her in, as snug as a bug in a rug, shut off the lights, and tiptoed out of the room.

Meaning: cozy and comfortable; safe and secure

Origin: For centuries writers have looked for clever ways to express feelings of warm comfort and contentment. In William Shakespeare's time (around the year 1600), people said "snug as pigs in pease-straw." But "snug as a bug in a rug" is a perfect expression because it contains three rhyming words. Benjamin Franklin used the phrase in a letter he wrote in 1772. The "bug" referred to was probably moth larvae or a carpet beetle peacefully snoozing inside a rolled-up rug (which in Franklin's time could have meant either a carpet or a blanket).

S

Soft-Soap

Maura thought that if she soft-soaped the teacher, he'd cancel the test.

Meaning: to try to persuade by flattery or gentle urging

Origin: This phrase comes from the first half of the 1800s when an imaginative writer saw a figurative similarity between slithery, slippery soft soap and insincere flattery and coaxing. Trying to get people to do what you want by sweet-talking them is like coating them with soft, smooth soap. A related expression is to "butter someone up" (see page 23).

Sow Your Wild Oats

"Can you believe that our quiet, dignified grandfather sowed his wild oats when he was just out of college?"

Meaning: to behave wildly and foolishly, especially when young

Origin: The wild oat that grows is actually a weed. It is useless and, since at least 194 B.C., has been correlated to young people frittering their time away with silly or reckless activities.

Spare the Rod and Spoil the Child

"I'm glad I wasn't brought up in the old days when 'spare the rod and spoil the child' was acceptable."

Meaning: to physically punish children when they misbehave so they'll learn to behave properly in the future

Origin: This call for strict discipline appears in various wordings at least six different times in the Bible. It made its way into English in about the year 1000. Corporal punishment (hitting or whipping) with a stick, cane, or paddle used to be a popular way to rear a child. It was legal for schoolmasters to do it not too long ago. The fear among parents was that if they "spared the rod" and didn't swat their offspring when he or she was bad, they would "spoil the child."

Spick-and-Span

"The counselor wanted the bunk spick-and-span before we could get our snacks."

Meaning: extremely clean, tidy, neat

Origin: There are two possible explanations about the origin of this famous phrase. One comes from the Old Norse language. "Spick" meant trim or neat. "Spanny" was a word that meant absolutely new. In the 1500s the two words might have been put together to mean "new and neat." Another theory comes from the days of the great sailing ships. "Spick" was a spike or nail. "Span" was a wood chip. A "spick and span new" ship (the original wording) was one on which every spike and chip was brand-new. By the mid-19th century this idiom was popular in the United States. Its popularity was helped by its alliteration (*spick-and-span*).

Spill the Beans

Don't spill the beans, but Adrienne is getting the art award.

Meaning: to give away a secret to someone who is not supposed to know it

Origin: A popular theory about the origin of this idiom goes back to the ancient Greeks and their secret societies. People voted you into these clubs by putting a white bean or a black bean into a jar (white = yes; black = no). The beans were supposed to be counted in secret, but if somebody accidentally (or purposefully) knocked over the jar and spilled the beans, the secret vote would be revealed. Another theory holds that this is an example of American slang from the early 1900s that combined two old words, "spill" (meaning "talk," from the 1500s) and "beans" (meaning "information," from the 1200s), into a new phrase. A related expression is "let the cat out of the bag" (see page 111).

Spitting Image

"You must be David's father. He's the spitting image of you."

Meaning: a perfect resemblance; an exact likeness

Origin: Originally this saying was "spit and image." ("Spit" was an old word that meant "likeness," but the original word might have been "spirit," shortened into "spit.") As the years went by, "spit and" was pronounced "spittin" and later became "spitting." The word seemed to fit because people said that a boy who looked a lot like his father could have been spit out of his father's mouth. Today, any relative can be the "spitting image" of any other relative. A related expression is "chip off the old block" (see page 34).

Split Hairs

"Aaron and his sister are always splitting hairs. He said there were forty-seven explosions in the movie; she said forty-six."

Meaning: to argue about small, unimportant differences

Origin: William Shakespeare used an expression similar to this in about 1600 in one of his plays, and "splitting hairs" has been widely used since the late 1600s. When the saying originated, it was thought to be impossible to split anything as fine as a hair.

Stick-in-the-Mud

"We wanted a giant-screen TV, but Dad said the little one was good enough. What a stick-in-the-mud."

Meaning: a person with old-fashioned ideas who avoids anything new, ignores progress, and fights change

Origin: Although the idea behind this idiom goes back at least 500 years, the exact phrase "stick-in-the-mud" was first heard in the early 1700s. It probably came from the image of a wagon stuck in the mud. Soon people started describing a dull, overly careful person as a "stick-in-the-mud."

Stick to Your Guns

You may be the only kid who thinks we need a longer school day, but I admire the way you stick to your guns.

Meaning: to stand firm and hold to one's position in the face of opposition; to stand up for your rights no matter what trouble you get into

Origin: At first this was a command to sailors manning the guns on military boats to stay at their posts even when the boat was besieged by enemies. Later, in the middle 1700s, the saying was extended to include anybody who persisted in holding onto his or her convictions. We usually have a good opinion of people who "stick to their guns," even if we don't always agree with them.

Stick Your Neck Out

"You shouldn't have to be the only one to complain. Why should you stick your neck out?"

Meaning: to take a bold or dangerous risk; to expose yourself to criticism

Origin: This 20th-century Americanism probably originated in the 1930s and referred to a chicken or turkey that got its neck stretched out when put on the chopping block.

Still Waters Run Deep

Antonia was a quiet student, but she was also brilliant. Still waters run deep.

Meaning: somebody can be more knowledgeable or emotional than he or she first appears to be; a silent person may be intelligent

Origin: This English proverb has been used since the 15th century. It's similar to expressions that have been used by people in other countries and that date back to the ancient Romans. It's based on a fact of nature: The shallow water in a river runs fast but deep water is usually calmer. This expression is sometimes applied to quiet people who you think are safe, but who may be dangerous plotters, spies, and saboteurs.

Stir Up a Hornet's Nest

"Please don't stir up a hornet's nest with your proposal to ban gum chewing in school."

Meaning: to make many people furious; to cause trouble

Origin: This popular saying originated in ancient Rome; by the 1700s people were saying it in English. There's a sensible warning that says, "Let sleeping dogs lie," (see page 111). "Don't stir up a hornet's nest" is a good piece of advice, too. Provoking a nest full of dangerous, stinging hornets would be foolish and dangerous. If you stir people up with your ideas or opinions, they might be as furious.

181

Straight from the Horse's Mouth

"I got it straight from the horse's mouth that there's going to be a pop quiz today."

Meaning: directly from the person or place that is the most reliable source or the best authority

Origin: If you want to know the age of a horse, you should examine the size and shape of its teeth. Someone trying to sell you a horse may say it's young, but if you get your information "straight from the horse's mouth," you should know for sure. This expression is relatively modern, dating only from the 1920s.

Straight from the Shoulder

This is straight from the shoulder: I don't want to room with you because you smoke.

Meaning: frankly, honestly

Origin: This is another well-known saying that comes from boxing. A prize fighter knows that a punch thrown straight from the shoulder is a full-force punch. It is quick, effective, and to the point. In the late 1800s this expression took on a wider meaning. If someone speaks to you in a sincere, honest way, even though it may upset you, he or she is speaking "straight from the shoulder." Other idioms that come from boxing are "hit below the belt" (see page 91), "on the ropes"(see page 135), and "pull no punches" (see page 151).

Straighten Up and Fly Right

"Learning to drive is serious business, so straighten up and fly right if you want your license."

Meaning: to stop behaving foolishly and start acting serious

Origin: This popular modern African-American expression could relate to birds or even airplanes. Instead of flying in a curved or crooked way, perhaps as a joke, the bird or pilot should readjust his flight pattern, straighten out his course, and fly directly to his destination. People who waste their time in aimless pursuits could be given the same advice, figuratively speaking. Stop fooling around and try to achieve your goal.

Straw that Broke the Camel's Back

"That last mistake was the straw that broke the camel's back."

Meaning: one final problem or misfortune that, added to previous troubles, proves more than a person can bear

Origin: In 1677 there appeared the expression, "the last feather that breaks the horse's back," which suggested that a horse could carry only so much weight on its back. If the weight of even one feather was added, it might make the horse collapse. Charles Dickens, the famous English novelist of the 1800s, changed that saying to "the straw that broke the camel's back," and today it means that people can take only so much trouble before they reach the limit of their endurance. One additional burden on top of many others might be all it takes to overwhelm a person. This idiom is so well known that it is often shortened to just the "last straw" or "final straw."

Strike a Happy Medium

"She wanted ice cream, but her father wanted cake, so they struck a happy medium. They bought an ice-cream cake."

Meaning: to find a compromise to a problem; to find a sensible solution midway between two opposite desires

Origin: To strike often means to hit upon something. The medium is the position that is midway between two extremes. So when people want different things, and they hit upon a compromise solution halfway between their opposite wishes, they've found a medium point that makes them both happy.

Strike while the Iron Is Hot

Emily's standing there all alone. Why not strike while the iron is hot and ask her to the dance?

Meaning: to act at the most favorable time or moment to get the best results; to take advantage of favorable conditions

Origin: This metaphor goes back to ancient times. Geoffrey Chaucer, a poet of the 1300s, was one of many English authors who used it. Blacksmiths all know that iron is most workable when it is red hot. In order to form the right shape on the anvil, the blacksmith has to strike while the iron is hot. A related saying is "make hay while the sun shines" (see page 119).

Stuffed Shirt

"The chairman of the board is such a stuffed shirt."

Meaning: a self-important person who shows a lot of phony dignity

Origin: Although William Shakespeare used a similar expression ("stuffed man"), the version with "shirt" is from the early 1900s. It suggests a person who has a falsely high opinion of his or her own worth and who shows it. People like that are puffed up with their own grandiose feelings about themselves. It's as if they're stuffed with exaggerated self-importance.

Swallow Hook, Line, and Sinker

Louie swallowed that story about the ghost hook, line, and sinker.

Meaning: to believe a story completely without questioning it; to be very gullible

Origin: This American expression from the 1800s may be based on an older British saying from the 1500s, "to swallow a gudgeon." A gudgeon is a small fish, like a minnow, that was often used as bait by fishermen. An unlucky fish usually swallows just the bait on the hook, but if it also swallows the fishing line and the lead sinker as well, it has gobbled up a lot. That's like a trusting person who accepts anything and everything he or she is told without thinking about whether or not it's true.

Swan Song

"We are going to the opera to hear Madame Scotto's swan song."

Meaning: the final, farewell performance of an actor or singer; one's last words or actions

Origin: In the myths of ancient Greece and in some poetry by William Shakespeare, you will find references to a swan that is mute or almost totally silent all its life, but that sings a lovely, sweet song just before it dies. In real life it doesn't happen that way (swans make sounds all their lives), but the story is nice and people enjoy it. Today, a performer's final appearance, an artist's last work, a scientist's last discovery, or an athlete's last game is often called a "swan song."

Sweep You off Your Feet

Maria married Carlos, her millionaire boss. She just swept him off his feet.

Meaning: to make a favorable impression; to affect with strong emotion or enthusiasm; to overcome someone with feelings of love or happiness so strong that he or she can't resist you

Origin: This idiom comes from the 19th century and joins a list of sayings that relate being overwhelmed by feelings of love with being knocked down: "She's a knockout"; "He bowled her over"; "They got carried away with each other." These expressions suggest that sometimes emotions are so intense that you can't even remain standing when you're hit by one of them.

Sweet Tooth

"With his sweet tooth, it will be nearly impossible for Jim to stay on a diet."

Meaning: a great desire to eat sweet foods, especially those with lots of sugar, such as jams, candies, and pastries

Origin: Even in the 1500s, when this famous idiom was first used, people loved sweets. This yearning was called having a "sweet tooth." Perhaps people thought that one tooth had a craving for salty foods, another for sour foods, and one for sweet foods. At first, "sweet tooth" referred to sweet meats, wines, and pastries, but today it is used to describe only a craving for cakes, pies, and other sugary foods.

Take a Backseat

"When it comes to pottery, I take a backseat to Shelly. She's a whiz."

Meaning: to be in an inferior position; to take second place to another person who is in control

Origin: This idiom became popular in the United States in the middle 1880s. It comes from being in the back seat of a vehicle. When you're in the driver's seat, you're the boss, and in control. When you're in the back seat, you're in a secondary position. It's like "playing second fiddle" (see page 147).

Take a Powder

"He saw the teacher he'd had an argument with in the restaurant, so he took a powder."

Meaning: to leave quickly; to sneak or run out of a place

Origin: Many people were using this expression in the United States by 1925. Earlier, they said, "dust out of here" or "take a run-out powder" to mean to depart in a rush. The "dust" in the earlier saying referred to the dust kicked up by one's shoes in running away. The expression may have changed to "powder" because of the explosiveness of gunpowder. If you flee so you won't get caught for something, you're "taking a powder."

Take a Shine to

Amazing. My mother really took a shine to my new pet iguana.

Meaning: to become fond of; to form a quick liking for someone or something

Origin: This American saying dates back to the 1880s and probably came from the earlier expression "to shine up to someone." That meant to behave nicely so someone will like you. Then they "take a shine" to you because of your appearance or personality. A similar saying is "to take a fancy to."

Take It to the Hoop

"He announced his candidacy for class president and took it to the hoop."

Meaning: to accomplish a project successfully; to do a great and thorough job

Origin: This modern African-American expression comes from the game of basketball. If a player gets possession of the ball and takes it all the way to the hoop and makes a basket, he or she is succeeding perfectly at what he or she set out to do. The saying is also applied to any area of life in which you carry out an undertaking all the way to its successful conclusion.

Take off Your Hat to Someone

Even with her arm in a sling, she cooked a marvelous meal. I have to take my hat off to her.

Meaning: to admire or praise someone for a notable accomplishment

Origin: In the middle of the 1800s, when this expression was born, many men wore hats. When a gentleman met a lady on the street, he tipped his hat as a gesture of respect. Today, even if you're not wearing a hat, you can say that you're "taking your hat off" to someone whose achievements you admire.

Take Someone under Your Wing

"Each senior will be assigned a freshman to take under his or her wing during the first month of school."

Meaning: to help, guide, or protect someone

Origin: The idea of a person offering protection to another person just as a mother bird takes her babies under the security of her wing was first mentioned in the Bible. In 1885 the famous Englishmen who wrote comic operas, Gilbert and Sullivan, further popularized the expression in a song from their musical *The Mikado*.

Take the Bitter with the Sweet

> The track meet was a bust, but you made a new friend. Learn to take the bitter with the sweet.

Meaning: to accept the bad things that happen along with the good

Origin: The famous English poet of the 14th century Geoffrey Chaucer first used this idea in one of his poems, and many other writers have since adopted the phrase. Of course, "bitter" represents bad happenings and "sweet" stands for good. Some people say that you have to take "the rough with the smooth," and that expression gets the message across just as effectively.

Take the Bull by the Horns

"Take the bull by the horns. March into the office and explain what happened."

Meaning: to act bravely in a troublesome situation; to face up to a difficult challenge by taking decisive action

Origin: For centuries daring bullfighters called matadors have been seizing bulls by the horns to wrestle them to the ground. It happens on ranches and in rodeos, too. By 1800 this brave, but risky, action had been expanded symbolically to other areas of life. The "bull" stood for any kind of trouble or challenge.

Take the Cake

"Ed's amazing triple play really took the cake."

Meaning: to deserve the highest award or prize

Origin: A cake has been a popular prize at contests for many centuries. In the time of the ancient Greeks, the winner of the cake was the person who could stay awake the longest at an all-night party. In the late 1800s in the United States, the cake winners were the couple judged best in a dance contest. (The winning dance was called the cakewalk.) Since then, this African-American saying has meant being the best in any endeavor.

Take with a Grain of Salt

Sally tends to exaggerate. Take what she says with a grain of salt.

Meaning: to not believe completely; to be doubtful

Origin: Some word experts think this expression first appeared in Latin by a Roman scholar in the 1st century B.C. The report was of the discovery of an antidote to poison: Take it with a grain of salt *(cum grano salis)*. Perhaps the saying refers to food that's not so tasty (like a story that's not so believable) being swallowed more easily with a little salt. Another possibility is that a single grain of salt isn't worth much, just like a story you don't think is completely true.

Talk through Your Hat

"Don't let what Eric said upset you. He's just talking through his hat."

Meaning: to talk nonsense; to say something without really knowing what you're talking about

Origin: The origin of this idiom is not clear. Some people think that if people really talked through their hats, they'd look ridiculous, like the nonsense they were saying. If people tell you that you're talking through your hat, they obviously don't have a high opinion of your words.

That's the Way the Ball Bounces

"You promised to baby-sit on the night of Dana's party? Oh, well, that's the way the ball bounces."

Meaning: that's the way life is; that's fate; things sometimes turn out a certain way and you can't do anything about it

Origin: This American idiom dates back to the 1950s. A similar idiom is "that's the way the cookie crumbles." The alliteration in both sayings (ball bounces, cookie crumbles) contributed to the word choices. This saying makes clear that unpredictable things often happen in life, and you have to learn to live with and accept them. The French have a similar saying, *C'est la vie* ("That's life.") We also say, "That's the way it goes."

Through the Grapevine

"She heard **through the grapevine** that she was being considered for a big promotion."

Meaning: through the informal spreading of messages, gossip, rumors, or other confidential information from one person to another

Origin: A grapevine is a long-stemmed plant that winds, climbs, and creeps from grape to grape to grape. In a similar way, news can travel from person to person to person, either spoken or written. This 20th-century African-American idiom could go as far back as the 1600s.

Throw a Curve

My boss **threw me a curve** when he said I'd have to work late the night of the basketball play-offs.

Meaning: to surprise someone in an unpleasant way; to mislead or lie

Origin: We get this expression from the American game of baseball in the 20th century. A tricky pitcher sometimes throws a curve ball that catches the batter off guard. This idiom can also mean lying to people to confuse or deceive them.

Throw a Monkey Wrench into the Works

"All the plans for the party were going smoothly until Tricia **threw a monkey wrench** into the works."

Meaning: to interfere with a smoothly running operation; to upset something in progress

Origin: In 1856 a tool was invented by a man named Monk and called Monk's wrench. Later the name was changed to monkey wrench. The sliding jaw of the tool reminded people of a monkey, and the nickname stuck. This American saying of the late 1800s presents the image of someone throwing a monkey wrench into machinery that's working perfectly and "gumming up the works" (see page 84).

Throw Caution to the Wind

"Pablo threw caution to the wind and went on the roller coaster."

Meaning: to be extremely daring; to take a huge risk; to act recklessly and hastily

Origin: The image of a brave person taking "caution" and fearlessly throwing it into the wind, where it's blown away, is an old one. We also use this expression to refer to the actions of a person who puts aside his or her fears to perform a brave deed.

Throw Cold Water on Something

"I was looking forward to my vacation until you threw cold water on it by saying the place is loaded with mosquitoes."

Meaning: to say or do something discouraging; to dampen one's enthusiasm for something

Origin: For thousands of years the best way to put out a fire was to douse it with water. If fire, heat, and warmth all represent enthusiasm, excitement, and passion, then cold water must stand for whatever lessens those emotions. So, if you throw cold water on someone's plans, you're a "wet blanket" (see page 204).

Throw in the Towel

You mustn't throw in the towel when the other team puts up great arguments.

Meaning: to give up; to admit that you're defeated; to quit

Origin: There are always towels or sponges near a boxing ring to wipe the sweaty boxers between rounds. In Britain, in the middle 1800s, the manager or friend of a boxer who was being badly beaten would often throw the towel or sponge into the boxing ring or up into the air as a signal of surrender. That meant the fight was over.

Throw the Baby Out with the Bathwater

"When John cleaned the garage, he threw away a new set of wrenches. That was throwing out the baby with the bathwater."

Meaning: to lose or throw out something valuable or useful when getting rid of something that is useless

Origin: This expression might have come from an old German proverb. By the turn of the 20th century, writers were using it in English. Imagine a parent who finishes bathing a baby in a tub and then throws the bathwater out with the baby still in it! That's like throwing away the most important part ("the baby") at the same time you're getting rid of whatever is not needed ("the bathwater").

Throw the Book at Someone

Dan was expelled for writing on the walls. They really threw the book at him.

Meaning: to punish severely for breaking rules or the law; to give the maximum penalty

Origin: In this idiom the "book" is the law book, filled with all the penalties that a judge can impose on the wrongdoer. Imagine a judge figuratively throwing that whole, heavy law book at an offender of the law, hitting him or her with the worst possible punishments. That image was in the mind of the writer who coined this expression many years ago.

Throw Your Hat into the Ring

"Dave threw his hat into the ring today. He's running for class secretary."

Meaning: to announce one's candidacy for election to office; to issue a challenge

Origin: Men used to challenge each other to prizefights in the United States in the early 19th century by taking off their hats and throwing them into a ring on the ground. That custom became the basis for this idiom. People who state that they are running for any elective office are "throwing their hats into the ring."

Throw Your Weight Around

That kid is the new school bully. He likes to throw his weight around.

Meaning: to use one's power in a mean, threatening way; to be bossy or rough

Origin: This popular saying from the early 1900s reminds us that big, heavy, or tall people can often be intimidating, especially if you're lightweight or short. Wrestlers, football players, and gangsters in movies are often heavyweights. So this saying came to mean to be bossy or tough.

Tickled Pink

"Bob was tickled pink when he got a Valentine from his dog."

Meaning: to be very amused or pleased; to be delighted, entertained, extremely happy

Origin: If you tickle someone, his or her face often turns pink. So, if someone is tickling you by doing or saying something so that you're giggling and your skin is getting reddish, then you're probably having a good time being "tickled pink." A similar expression is "tickled someone's fancy."

Tickle Your Funny Bone

"Jessica's hilarious antics always tickle my funny bone."

Meaning: to make you laugh; to amuse somebody

Origin: There's a bone in your upper arm at the back of your elbow that has the Latin name "humerus." Since that sounds like "humorous," people have been calling it the "funny bone" for many years. If you accidentally bump it, the sensitive nerve in your elbow tingles as if electricity were running through it. If you laugh at a joke, then, according to this expression, it's tickling your funny bone. (Sometimes the funny bone is called the "crazy bone.")

Tied to Someone's Apron Strings

"You can't be tied to your mother's apron strings all your life."

Meaning: to be dependent on someone, such as one's mother; to not be able to do anything without asking your mother

Origin: Years ago many women stayed home to work and care for the children and house. To keep their clothes clean, they wore aprons tied in the back with strings. If a grown man was controlled by his mother, it was often said that he was "tied to his mother's apron strings." Later, if he was under the strong influence of his wife, he was tied to her apron strings.

Tighten Your Belt

"Sonny's boss won't give him a pay raise but his rent went up. Now he has to tighten his belt."

Meaning: to live on less money; to make sacrifices and lower one's standard of living

Origin: If you have less money to spend, you'll probably buy less food. If you eat less, you'll probably lose weight. If you lose weight, you'll have to tighten your belt. That's what the person who created this saying had in mind.

Till the Cows Come Home

I'll stand here till the cows come home unless you pay me back the money I lent you.

Meaning: for a long, long time

Origin: This late 16th-century idiom probably refers to how cows take their sweet time to return from the fields to the barn. When you use this expression, you're describing a long passage of time using a barnyard image.

Tip of the Iceberg

"In chemistry, learning the symbols for the elements is just the tip of the iceberg."

Meaning: just a small part of a larger problem or a worse situation

Origin: An iceberg is a huge body of ice that has broken away from a glacier and is floating in the ocean. The "tip of the iceberg" is a well-known 20th-century metaphor that points out that the top is only a tiny part of a mountain of floating ice. An estimated 90 percent of an iceberg is hidden underwater.

Tongue-in-Cheek

Don't be insulted by what Roz said. She meant it tongue-in-cheek.

Meaning: intended as a joke; not serious; insincere; mocking

Origin: This phrase may have been made up by an English humorist in the mid-1800s. You would have difficulty saying anything with your tongue in your cheek. Some people actually do poke their cheek with their tongue after making an insincere remark to show they were only kidding. It's a facial expression similar to winking after saying something that's meant to be taken as a joke.

Too Big for Your Britches

"I used to like George when he was a little kid, but now I think he's grown too big for his britches."

Meaning: conceited; swelled with self-importance; haughty

Origin: This is an old American expression that goes back more than 200 years. Britches (also spelled "breeches") is an old word for pants. If a person swelled with feelings of self-importance, he or she might burst right out of his or her clothes. Another version of this saying is "too big for your boots." A related idiom that captures the same puffed-up-with-self-worth idea is "stuffed shirt" (see page 184). Of course, you could also be rightfully proud of yourself or a loved one, and therefore be "bursting at the seams."

Too Many Cooks Spoil the Broth

The decorations look terrible because the committee couldn't agree on anything. Too many cooks spoil the broth.

Meaning: a project is set back rather than helped by too many organizers; the more people who work on one project, the worse it will turn out

Origin: This old proverb goes back to the 1500s. The creator of this saying knew that one master chef can create a delicious meal. But if a whole bunch of people try to cook the meal at the same time, the food (broth) is sure to be ruined.

Top Banana

"Since the early days of vaudeville, Uncle Henny has been a top banana."

Meaning: the leading comedian in a variety show; a boss

Origin: Some word experts think this phrase may have started with an old comedy routine involving the sharing of bananas, but nobody is really sure. Today people call the chief comic in a musical comedy or television show the "top banana." Some people may also use the term humorously to refer to the boss in any group.

Top Drawer

"Aunt Shirley always takes the family out to some top-drawer restaurant."

Meaning: the highest quality; the best

Origin: The most likely origin of this 20th-century phrase is the top drawer of a dresser or bureau. Many people put their jewelry and other valuable possessions in the top drawer so that they can get them easily. From that custom comes this expression, which is used to describe people of the highest social status or anything that's the best in rank or quality.

Touch and Go

"It was touch and go for a while, but the vet says my rabbit will live."

Meaning: very risky, uncertain, or critical

Origin: This saying was first used in the 1800s and may have come from ships that came close to touching the bottom of the sea while in shallow water, or to touching other things that could sink them. These dangerous situations sometimes ended with narrow escapes. If the ship touched bottom but managed to go on, it had survived a "touch-and-go" situation. The term also referred to horse-drawn carriages, when there was a narrow escape from an accident after the wheels of two coaches touched. Today we use this phrase to describe any uncertain situation that could end either horribly or happily.

Touch Something with a Ten-Foot Pole

I won't touch that controversy with a ten-foot pole.

Meaning: to avoid at all costs; to stay far away from a difficult problem

Origin: A writer in the mid-1800s wanted a lively way to describe someone who didn't want to deal with a troublesome issue. The image of a person not wanting to touch something nasty even with a pole ten feet long came to mind, and this famous idiom was created. This saying is sometimes "touch something with a ten-foot bargepole." It is always used in the negative, with words such as won't, wouldn't, or don't, because it refers to something you don't want to have anything to do with.

Trip the Light Fantastic

"Those kids in Mrs. Keys's tap-dance class really know how to trip the light fantastic."

Meaning: to dance

Origin: John Milton, the great English poet of the 1600s, made up this phrase in his poem "L'Allegro" in 1632. Readers thought that the phrase "trip the light fantastic" was a delightful way to describe dancing, and more than 360 years later, we're still using it.

True-Blue

"The true-blue supporters of our team cheer for us even when we lose."

Meaning: very loyal, dependable, and faithful

Origin: This expression comes from an old proverb and has at least two possible origins. In the 17th century, blue was the color of many British groups: Scottish Covenanters, the Whig party, and even the varsity teams at Oxford and Cambridge universities. Anyone loyal and true to those groups wore something blue. Blue was also known as a true color because the blue thread made in Coventry, England, during the Middle Ages was highly regarded for holding its color. The blue dye didn't run, and so blue came to stand for faithfulness. Note also that "true" and "blue" rhyme, and rhymes often help an idiom become more widely used.

Turn over a New Leaf

"If you haven't been feeling fit, maybe it's time to turn over a new leaf and start exercising."

Meaning: to correct one's behavior or attitude; to begin anew; to make a fresh start

Origin: In the 16th century, when this idiom was born, people referred to pages in a book as leaves. "Turning over a leaf" meant turning to a blank page in a workbook to begin a new lesson. What the expression suggested was that you can change your behavior for the future and begin again as if turning a new page in the book of your life.

Turn the Other Cheek

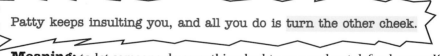

Patty keeps insulting you, and all you do is turn the other cheek.

Meaning: to let someone do something bad to you and not defend yourself or hit back; to meekly ignore abuse or injury

Origin: This is a Biblical expression. In the New Testament, Jesus urged his followers to refuse revenge when someone provoked, insulted, or physically hurt them. If someone slapped you on one side of your face, you should not fight back with angry words or blows. Instead, be patient and turn your head to the other side.

198

Turn the Tables

"Notre Dame was beating us badly, but then we turned the tables on them and won!"

Meaning: to reverse the situation; to make the opposite happen

Origin: This saying probably came from the early 1600s and has two possible origins. In some tabletop board games such as chess, checkers, and backgammon, the table was actually turned as part of the play. There were also tables that had two-sided tops. One side was polished smooth and used for eating; the other side was rougher and used for working on. You would turn the tabletop over when you needed to. Now when you "turn the tables" on someone, you're causing a complete reversal in the situation, usually to your advantage.

Turn up Your Nose at Someone

"Since Barbara moved to the city, she turns up her nose at her old pals."

Meaning: to regard something with haughtiness; to be snobby; to show that someone or something is not good enough for you

Origin: Even in the 1500s, when this idiom was created, people showed scorn for things they considered beneath them by sneering or putting their noses in the air in a snooty way. That arrogant facial expression created the saying "turn your nose up," because that's what people did if they thought they were better than everyone else.

Two-Faced

How can you trust her? Vera's two-faced, if you ask me.

Meaning: false; dishonest

Origin: This expression comes from Roman mythology. The god Janus was the keeper of the gates of heaven. He had two faces so that he could be a better watchman. (It's like the expression, "two heads are better than one.") In the early 1600s a writer referred to someone who was a double-crosser as "two-faced." This captured the image of a lying person who tells you one thing and then tells your friend something else, or who smiles at you and then criticizes you to others.

Under the Table

"The boxer was accused of accepting money under the table to lose the fight."

Meaning: in secret, dishonestly; not out in the open

Origin: Sometimes people who wanted to unlawfully influence public officials passed money under the table (not out in the open) as a bribe or payoff. Cheating card players often slipped cards under the table to their partners. During Prohibition in the United States (1920–33) selling liquor was illegal, but people could buy it secretly under the counter (where the police couldn't see). During World War II, the sale of many daily items was rationed (strictly limited), but some shopkeepers kept things under the counter (not out on the shelves) for their friends and relatives. So from many sources, the phrase "under the table" has come to describe any dishonest transactions done on the sly. An idiom that has the same meaning is "under the counter."

Under the Weather

Ms. Capers will not be in today. She's feeling a little under the weather.

Meaning: sick; not well; in trouble with money

Origin: In the mid-1700s many people in the United States traveled by boat. In stormy weather, when the water was rough, a lot of people got seasick and were said to be suffering under the influence of bad weather. Soon the phrase was shortened to just "under the weather." The saying first appeared in a novel in 1850.

Up a Creek Without a Paddle

"Holly lost her costume, and the play is tonight. She's up a creek without a paddle."

Meaning: in deep trouble and unable to do anything about it; in serious trouble

Origin: Imagine being in a rowboat on a river or creek far from home and you lose your oar! That's the picture painted by this early 20th-century idiom.

Up Against the Wall

"Ben's up against the wall. He lost his job and can't make the payments on the house."

Meaning: in big trouble; in a difficult or desperate situation

Origin: This example of American slang from the late 19th century probably refers to the practice of lining people up against walls for a variety of reasons. Suspected criminals stand against a wall in a police lineup. The police often make a person being arrested lean forward with his or her hands up against a wall. A robber may also hold his or her prey at gunpoint up against a wall to prevent the victim from escaping.

Upper Crust

"The poor student fell hopelessly in love with a girl from the upper crust."

Meaning: high society; social or financial elite; important people

Origin: This expression began to be widely used in the mid-1800s. The upper crust of a loaf of bread was considered the best, tastiest part. "Upper crust" came to mean the best class of people, the most elite in society, those with the highest intellectual, social, or economic status.

Upset the Applecart

Don't let Barry know about our plans for the ski trip or he'll upset the applecart.

Meaning: to spoil or interfere with a plan; to obstruct progress; to mess everything up by surprise or accident

Origin: From ancient Roman times comes this famous saying, although the Romans just said "cart." "Apple" was added to "cart" in the late 1800s because it helped create a metaphor for ruining something that was carefully arranged. Imagine a farmer or a vendor pushing a large cart piled high with apples on the way to market. Along comes some clumsy oaf who knocks over the cart and spills all the apples. The farmer's plan to sell his apples is spoiled.

Waiting for the Other Shoe to Drop

"Yesterday was part one of our exam, and now we're waiting for the other shoe to drop."

Meaning: to do something that completes an action; to wait in suspense for something to be finished

Origin: The man who lives in the apartment above you is getting ready for bed. He takes off one shoe and drops it noisily on the floor. You wait anxiously below for the other shoe to drop; then you can fall asleep in peace and quiet. A 20th-century writer created this expression.

Walk on Eggs

Jen was walking on eggs when she tried to return the necklace she had borrowed without asking.

Meaning: to be very cautious; to proceed warily

Origin: This saying first appeared in Italy in the late 1500s. The writer who came up with the idiom must have had the following image in mind: A person stepping very carefully on a floor of eggs trying not to break a single shell. It can't be done, of course, even with hard-boiled eggs, but it gets across the idea of doing something with great caution.

Walking on Air

"When she found out that she was having a baby, Nancy left the doctor's office walking on air."

Meaning: to be exuberantly happy, excited, and joyful

Origin: This 20th-century expression plays on the idea that feeling down means you're sad or depressed, while feeling up means you're cheerful and glad. What's the highest you can be? Up in the air, of course. Similar idioms that equate being in the air with being happy are "on cloud nine" (see page 131) and "on top of the world" (see page 136).

Wash Your Hands of Something

I'm tired of arguing with my lab partners, so I'm washing my hands of the science project.

Meaning: to withdraw from something; to end one's association or responsibility for something; to disavow, disclaim, or disown

Origin: This expression comes from the Bible. Pontius Pilate, a Roman official in Judea, announced that he could not save Jesus from being executed. He then washed his hands right in front of a crowd of people, saying that he was not guilty of Jesus' death. When you "wash your hands of something," you're not actually at a sink with soap and water. You're just saying that it's not your responsibility, or you don't want to be involved further.

Watched Pot Never Boils

"Waiting for the mail carrier isn't going to make the letter come any sooner. A watched pot never boils."

Meaning: when waiting anxiously or impatiently for something to happen, it seems to take much longer

Origin: If you put a fire under a pot of water, it will eventually boil, of course. But if you just stand there and watch the pot, it will seem to take forever for the boiling bubbles to first appear. Anxiety and impatience do not speed things up; they make them seem slower.

Water over the Dam

"Lost your ring last week? It's water over the dam now."

Meaning: something that is past and cannot be changed

Origin: Sometimes people say it's "water under the bridge," but wherever the water is going, once it has flowed on, it cannot come back. That's why an irretrievable, irreversible situation is described with this watery expression.

Wear Your Heart on Your Sleeve

"Everyone in the school knows Mel is in love with Ellen, because he wears his heart on his sleeve."

Meaning: to show one's emotions and feelings openly

Origin: William Shakespeare used this expression in his famous tragedy *Othello* around the year 1600. In those days, it was the custom for a young lady to tie a ribbon around the arm of her boyfriend. The boy then wore this favor on his sleeve, one of the most visible parts of his clothing, to display the feelings of his heart for all the world to see. Today, the feelings that you reveal by "wearing your heart on your sleeve" are often of love, but they could be another emotion too.

Wet Behind the Ears

"Lisa wouldn't hire him as a manager because he was too wet behind the ears."

Meaning: young, inexperienced, and immature

Origin: When a baby colt or calf is first born, it's wet all over with birth fluid. It quickly starts to dry, but the little indentation behind its ears stays wet the longest. Farmers always knew this, but some word experts think that in the early 20th century, officers in the American armed forces began using this barnyard expression to describe new soldiers. The saying is also a reference to a young animal that was washed by its mother.

Wet Blanket

I hope Terry doesn't come to the amusement park with us—he's such a wet blanket.

Meaning: a person who spoils other people's fun by being depressing, dull, sour, nagging, or humorless

Origin: This is an early 19th-century expression. Native Americans and others often put out their campfires with blankets they had dipped in the nearest river. If fire represents enthusiasm, excitement, passion, and joy, then the wet blanket that puts out the fire stands for a pessimist or spoilsport. A person acting like that will rain on your parade.

What's Good for the Goose
Is Good for the Gander

"If the girls team can't travel to the championship, neither should the boys team. What's good for the goose is good for the gander."

Meaning: a rule or method of treatment that applies to one person or group must also apply to others, especially your mate

Origin: A gander is a male goose, and according to this saying, what's appropriate for the female of the species is appropriate for the male, too. At first it may have been a call for equality between the sexes, but today "goose" and "gander" don't stand for "female" and "male" so much as any one person and another person. And "good" in this idiom can have a negative meaning.

Wheel and Deal

Sasha's uncle is an international businessman who wheels and deals all over the world.

Meaning: to skillfully and aggressively make big plans with important business, usually to earn a lot of money

Origin: The slang expression for an important person is "big wheel." A "wheeler-dealer" is an important person who makes substantial deals. The saying originated in gambling houses of the American West, where there were gamblers who were heavy betters at cards ("deal") and roulette ("wheel"). Sometimes this phrase refers to people who are big-time operators in tricky, perhaps dishonest, ways.

When the Cat's Away, the Mice Will Play

"When the counselor left, we had a pillow fight. When the cat's away the mice will play."

Meaning: when the person in charge is absent, people will usually do as they please and take advantage of the freedom

Origin: This proverb appears in many languages and has been in use in English since the 1600s. If there's a cat in the house, the mice will tend to stay hidden. But if the cat is gone, the mice will feel safer and venture out. It's the same with people. When the authority figure (the "cat") is not there, the people being supervised (the "mice") run free.

Where there's Smoke, there's Fire

"Kelly bought a new can of spray paint the day the graffiti appeared. She must have done it. Where there's smoke, there's fire."

Meaning: there is always a basis for a rumor, no matter how untrue it appears; suspicious things usually mean that something is wrong

Origin: In some form or other, this expression has been around since at least 43 B.C., and started getting popular in the mid-1500s. There can never be a fire without some smoke. In this metaphorical saying, the smoke represents the suspicious clues to some wrongdoing and the fire is the dirty deed itself. So when there's evidence that something bad happened, it probably did.

White Elephant

There's a white-elephant sale on Saturday. Bring all your junk to sell.

Meaning: any possession that is useless, unwanted, or costs a lot of money to keep

Origin: There is a legend that in ancient Siam (now Thailand) a king once gave a rare white elephant to a person at his court whom he didn't like. Sounds like a nice gift, but the white elephant was considered sacred, couldn't be made to do any work, and cost a fortune to feed and tend. The courtier couldn't get rid of this big drain on his money because it was a gift from the king. In a short time, the unfortunate man was poor. That's probably what the king intended. The expression first was used in English in the late 1800s.

Wild-Goose Chase

"It's a wild-goose chase trying to discover who gave you this cold."

Meaning: a useless or hopeless search, especially because something does not exist or can't be found

Origin: William Shakespeare used this famous phrase in his play *Romeo and Juliet,* and it's been widely used since about 1600. It's practically impossible to catch a wild goose. It's like trying to capture a greased pig or find a "needle in a haystack" (see page 124). It also may refer to a kind of horse race in which each horse had to follow the erratic course of the leader. Such a race looks like wild geese following the leader in formation.

With Flying Colors

As expected, Peggy passed her tests with flying colors.

Meaning: with ease and great success; in triumph

Origin: Sometimes a naval ship or other vessel will sail into a port with many colorful flags (its "colors") gloriously flying from its masts. What a thrilling sight! That image was extended to describe people who do something marvelous and spectacularly successful.

Without Batting an Eyelash

"Deepa accepted the award without batting an eyelash."

Meaning: without showing emotion or interest; impassive

Origin: To "bat" an eye was a way of saying "blink" in the early 1900s when this phrase first appeared. Usually a person who sees, hears, or experiences something unusual, scary, or fantastic will show some feeling, or at least blink. If that person is so cool, calm, and collected that he or she doesn't even bat an eyelash, then there's no outward show of emotion at all.

Wolf in Sheep's Clothing

"The new landlord acts friendly, but he might be a wolf in sheep's clothing."

Meaning: somebody who appears to be harmless but is really dangerous

Origin: The idea behind this saying appears in one of Aesop's fables and in the New Testament (Matthew 7:15). When most people think of a wolf, they think of a dangerous animal. A sheep is thought of as friendly, gentle, and harmless. So if a wicked wolf wanted to fool people into thinking he was a nice guy, he might disguise himself in a sheep costume.

Word of Mouth

> The movie got bad reviews, but it became popular by word of mouth.

Meaning: by one person telling another; by speaking, rather than writing

Origin: If people see something they like or don't like, such as a movie, TV show, play, or book, and they tell their friends about it, the news is being spread by "word of mouth" instead of by television commercials, newspaper advertising, billboards, and other kinds of publicity.

Worth Your Salt

"In order to get a raise, you have to prove that you're worth your salt."

Meaning: deserving the pay or reward that you get

Origin: This 19th-century expression comes from an ancient practice. For thousands of years, salt, a common thing today, was rare and highly prized. The Roman army paid part of a soldier's wages in salt. Our word "salary" comes from the Latin word *salarium,* which means "salt money." So if you were a good, loyal, brave, hardworking soldier, you were worth what they paid you—salt. Now all hardworking employees are "worth their salt," regardless of how they're paid.

Wrong Side of the Tracks

"Alex's mother was horrified when he started dating a girl from the wrong side of the tracks."

Meaning: from a less socially desirable part of town; the poor, unfashionable

Origin: In the early days of the railroads, about the middle of the 1800s, train tracks often divided a town into rich and poor sections. The better-off neighborhoods were sometimes built on the side of town where the smoke from trains didn't blow. So the "wrong side of the tracks" was a phrase that came to describe the socially and economically undesirable part of town.

You Can Lead a Horse to Water but You Can't Make Him Drink

"We gave him a new shirt, but he still wears the ripped one. You can lead a horse to water, but you can't make him drink."

Meaning: you can encourage, but not force, someone to do something

Origin: This expression was first used in the 12th century, when riding a horse was the main way of traveling long distances. A horse owner knew that an animal needed to drink water, especially after a long ride on a hot day. But even though you could take your horse right to the banks of a cool, fresh spring, that didn't mean the stubborn horse would drink. For centuries that truth has been applied to people who do what they want to even though you try to persuade them otherwise.

You Can't Teach an Old Dog New Tricks

I tried to give Grandma my new recipe for spaghetti sauce, but she refused. You can't teach an old dog new tricks.

Meaning: people who find it difficult or impossible to change their ways or adjust to new ideas

Origin: This is an old proverb based on some truth. Animal trainers have known for centuries that it's best to try to train an animal when it's young and not too set in its ways. An older animal likes doing things a certain way and will resist new methods.

ALPHABETICAL INDEX

214

J

K

L

M

KEY WORD INDEX

A

B

222

227

228

G

H

230

231

M

239

T

242